At War with the Word

At War with the Word

Literary Theory and Liberal Education

R.V. Young

ISI Books

INTERCOLLEGIATE STUDIES INSTITUTE
WILMINGTON, DELAWARE
1999

Cataloging-in-Publication Data

Young, R. V., 1947-
    At war with the word : literary theory and liberal education / by R.V. Young.—1st ed.—Wilmington, DE : ISI Books, 1999.

       p. cm.

    Includes bibliographical references and index.
    ISBN 1-882926-27-7
    1. New Criticism. 2. Criticism—History—20th Century.
    3. American Literature—History and Criticism—Theory, etc.
    4. English Literature—History and Criticism—Theory, etc. I. Title.

PN98 .N4 Y68 1999   99-71452
801 / .95—dc21   CIP

Published in the United States by:
    ISI Books
    Post Office Box 4431
    Wilmington, DE 19807-0431

Manufactured in the United States of America

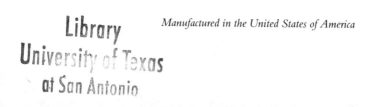

In Memoriam,
William K. Wimsatt, Jr.
1907–1975

Scribendi recte sapere est et principium et fons.

Contents

Preface

The following chapters began as presentations for a variety of academic audiences and subsequently appeared, as revised for publication, in several different journals. Despite this heterogeneity of origin and a process of composition that occurred intermittently over a fifteen-year period, this volume is not a collection of discrete essays, but a book comprising chapters that develop different facets of a single argument. What has always united the various pieces in this book, even as separate essays, is the conviction that the emerging dominance of postmodernist theory in departments of English and foreign language in America results from indifference and often outright hostility to literature as such. The power of great literature is generated by its capacity to provide a model of human experience that engages us imaginatively and emotionally as well as intellectually. Like the other fine arts, literature furnishes men and women with a knowledge of themselves that is immediate and concrete while at the same time, paradoxically, the object of disinterested contemplation. The thesis of this book is, then, that the moral realism of great literature makes it more than an amusement or a popular diversion and worthy of study by the most sophisticated academic resources.

Postmodernist theories of literature, whatever their differences, are all forms of reductivism: they deny to imaginative literature its unique status among other forms of discourse. Works of literature, which render an imaginative and coherent account of some phase of human experience, which confer independent meaning on the human condition, are an affront to the materialism and nihilism of contemporary academic ideologies. Postmodern theories offer less a new interpretive approach to literature than a means of putting it in its place as simply another social or economic phenomenon to be mastered by technical expertise. The dominant versions of contemporary literary theory thus pose a threat to liberal education. As a representation of human experience, imaginative literature is arguably the central subject of the humanities insofar as it acquaints us most powerfully and intimately with our humanity. Such is the argument of Sir Philip Sidney's *Defence of Poetry*, and his case is strengthened by the prominence in any liberal arts curriculum of works written as philosophy, history, or biography that assume a second life as literature: the Socratic dialogues of Plato, Gibbon's *Decline and Fall*, Boswell's *Life of Johnson*. Although such works may be technically superseded as sources of information, they remain indispensable for their qualities of style and imaginative vigor, which are particularly literary virtues. Such features both enact and remind us of our specifically *human nature*, with its measure of rational and spiritual freedom from the constraints of the material order. An education in the humanities is a *liberal* education precisely because liberty and its concomitant responsibility are the hallmarks of what is distinctively human. In denying the uniqueness of literature as an imaginative representation of human experience that transcends any merely empirical or analytic account, postmodernism denies the uniqueness of humanity itself. Men and women are no more than clever, complicated, relatively hairless primates whose nature and origin are theoretically reducible to the laws of physics, and whose actual identity is a matter of social construction—the fragile fabrication of converging economic and cultural forces. It has been my purpose to reassert the singular value of literary study in the enterprise of liberal education and thereby to indicate that the affirmation of human dignity is at the heart of our culture.

Chapter One maintains that the virulent attack that has been mounted against the New Criticism over the past 30 years is more than a merely academic dispute. It is, rather, an ideological assault that depends upon misrepresentation of the New Critics, and that aims as much at diminishing the value and influence of literature as such. Chapter Two is a critique of deconstruction as developed by its most prominent exponent, Jacques Derrida. Although the glamor of deconstruction has faded somewhat in the past 15 years, it remains indispensable to postmodernism because no other mode of analyzing discourse furnishes such a plausible guise for the nihilistic assumptions that energize contemporary literary theory. Chapter Three deals with three different versions of deconstruction in the work of Derrida's ally, Paul de Man, of his rival, the psychoanalyst Jacques Lacan, and of the maverick American critic, Harold Bloom. Although the writings of these three men vary enormously in tone and effect, all three share a common distaste for the creaturely status of men and women and a denial of the fundamental limits of human nature. The result is a criticism less concerned to interpret works of literature than to reconstruct literature as a vehicle for imposing the critic's own will upon a recalcitrant reality. Chapter Four takes up the New Historicism, which, along with associated movements such as cultural materialism and feminism, is often now regarded as the chief successor to deconstruction. This chapter argues that, despite the New Historicism's more explicit preoccupation with political and cultural power and its economic determinism, it depends, finally, on deconstruction's undermining of logic and the concept of nature. Chapter Five, focusing on Stanley Fish, America's most visible professor of English, explores the parallels between contemporary literary theory and recent controversies regarding the interpretation of the Constitution. Here the connection between irresponsible academic theorizing and destructive legal and social policy is demonstrated. Finally, Chapter Six considers various approaches to literary instruction—both promising and dubious—and concludes that the essential justification for the role of literature in liberal education is the excellence of literature in illuminating our vision of human nature and experience.

I have accumulated a good many intellectual and spiritual debts over the years that this book has been taking shape. Most of the chapters began as talks presented to various groups of university faculty and students, and I am grateful for the hospitality and the thoughtful responses that I was afforded on these occasions. The initial versions of Chapters 3-6 appeared in *Modern Age* and *The Intercollegiate Review*, both published by the Intercollegiate Studies Institute. An early version of Chapter 1 appeared in *First Things* and of Chapter 2 in the Proceedings of the Fellowship of Catholic Scholars; I am grateful to the editors for permission to reuse this material. Jeff Nelson of the Intercollegiate Studies Institute first suggested this book to me, and his efforts have been ably seconded by Brooke Daley and Sam Torode. Many friends and colleagues have provided sympathy and advice, and I especially wish to mention Anne Gardiner and her late husband, Tom, Richard Harp, Anthony Low, Phoebe Spinrad, Stanley Stewart, and, above all, my colleagues Tom Hester and Brian Blackley. The dedication to William K. Wimsatt, Jr., is a tribute to one of the greatest literary theorists of the twentieth century with whom I had the privilege of studying many years ago.

R. V. Young, 17 January 1999

CHAPTER ONE

The Old New Criticism
and Its Critics

The pugnacious practitioners of academic literary studies agree about very little, but there is one consensus: the New Criticism—that is, the *old* New Criticism associated with the names of T. S. Eliot, Allen Tate, John Crowe Ransom, Cleanth Brooks—*that* New Criticism is over, finished, defunct. What is more, this shift in critical fashion is widely perceived not merely as a routine scholarly development, but as a great liberation or the lifting of an onerous burden. A newcomer to the scene might surmise that literature professors had been bearing the entire weight of *The World's Body* upon their shoulders, or that textbooks like *Understanding Poetry* and *Sound and Sense* constituted a form of bondage or an imposition upon the innocent credulity of English department faculties.[1] Never again, they seem to proclaim, with a collective sigh of relief and the smug tone of a man conscious of having recovered righteousness, will we submit to that unhistorical *formalism* or subject our students to the cultural *elitism* of closely explicating "canonical works." Everywhere the atmosphere of classrooms and library bookstack carrels thickens with an almost palpable fog of sanctimony.

Now considered objectively, this is a very strange state of affairs. The New Criticism flourished during the thirties, forties, and fifties and remained influential even through the sixties when its dominance over literary study was everywhere challenged. During this time the study of literature in the modern vernacular languages was firmly established in the curricula of American universities; English and American literature, in particular, assumed a central role in undergraduate education and became a major focus of graduate training and academic scholarship. It is not too much to say that the achievements of the New Critics and their followers staked out the literary field and defined the university environment in which the revisionists now operate. If the movement known as the New Criticism had never occurred, it is improbable that the position and activities of literary scholars would be of much significance in contemporary higher education. Whatever shortcomings may have emerged in the New Critical program, whatever defects or excesses of method or substance may have stood in need of correction, one would expect the beneficiaries of the achievements of the New Criticism to regard it with at least an affectionate tolerance. Hence the current attitude among the denizens of English and foreign language departments, which ranges from severe disapproval to scathing repudiation, is more than a little surprising.

It is still more surprising when one realizes that the condemnation of the New Criticism is founded on misconceptions if not outright deceptions. In *The Attack on Literature* René Wellek has demonstrated conclusively and with breathtaking ease that the major accusations leveled at the New Criticism are "baseless." Wellek lists four common allegations against the New Critics: (1) that they are "formalists" with no interest in the human content of literature; (2) that they ignore the historical context of literature; (3) that they reduce literature to an abstract science; and (4) that the "close reading" practiced by the New Critics is a mere pedagogical device, an American version of *explication de texte*, fit only for American undergraduates in provincial colleges. Wellek is astounded by such allegations: "They can be so convincingly refuted by an appeal to the texts that I wonder whether current commentators have ever actually read the writings of the New Critics."[2]

My own experience tends to corroborate Wellek's suspicion: more of the "current commentators" have probably read Frank Lentricchia or Jonathan Culler inveighing against the New Critics than have actually read the New Critics themselves. A good example is Linda Hutcheon's book about irony, which purports to treat irony as a "political issue" and worries about irony as a tool of "elitism."[3] Hutcheon treats Cleanth Brooks with disdain, quoting a dismissive passage by Jonathan Culler on Brooks's supposed misuse of the idea of context in explaining irony;[4] however, Hutcheon herself calls for a "new" understanding of irony that is "inclusive and relational: the said and the unsaid coexist for the interpreter, and each has meaning in relation to the other because they literally 'interact'...to create the real 'ironic' meaning. The 'ironic' meaning is not, then, simply the unsaid meaning, and the unsaid is not always a simple inversion or opposite of the said."[5] This is a fine understanding of irony, but it is hardly an innovation. In a classic 1949 essay, Cleanth Brooks describes irony as "a dynamic structure—a pattern of thrust and counterthrust"; and after listing apparently contradictory implications in a poem by Randall Jarrell, Brooks argues that what results is not incoherence, but a complex of ironic tension:

> None of these meanings cancels out the others. All are relevant, and each meaning contributes to the total meaning. Indeed, there is not a facet of significance which does not receive illumination from the figure.[6]

Brooks thus succeeded in devising a fully "relational" and "inclusive" conception of irony when his most patronizing critics were still in diapers.

This kind of ignorant presumption could be merely dismissed were it not so infectious. In a book published a year after Hutcheon's, Heather Dubrow credits Hutcheon with furnishing a "new" understanding of irony that opens up new possibilities for the interpretation of John Donne:

> The usual interpretation of irony…would confirm the assumption that when Donne's speakers appear to be expressing Petrarchan sentiments, the poem really discredits Petrarchism. Yet irony, as Linda Hutcheon argues, should be seen instead as inclusive in the sense that both meanings are experienced, as is the third meaning that is formed by the relationship between them.[7]

This passage provides less a discussion of irony than an example of it in its "usual" negative sense: Dubrow employs Hutcheon's "new" idea of irony to construct a reading of Donne that is, as we shall see further on in this chapter, a pallid imitation of Cleanth Brooks's groundbreaking interpretation half a century earlier.

It is doubtful, however, whether it would make any difference if Wellek's "current commentators" on the New Critics *did* bother to read them. The attack on the New Critics is not a mistake; that is, it is not based on a misunderstanding that could be cleared up to the satisfaction of all parties by a candid exchange of views. The New Criticism has not been vilified because of its errors and vices, which doubtless afflict it as all things human; it has been scourged for its virtues. It is not too much to say that the New Critics have been the victims of what used to be called in counterespionage circles a campaign of disinformation. The charge that comes up again and again

in current discussions of the New Criticism is *formalism*, "an opprobrious term," Wellek notes, "used first by Marxists against a group
of Russian scholars in the twenties."[8]

The contemporary academic scene is steeped in Marxism (even
though it is often unconscious), and "formalism" is the inevitable
dismissive term in discussions of the New Criticism, even though
it often seems to comprise a range of mutually contradictory accusations. The fundamental implication of the term is that the New
Critics were concerned about literature only as an objectified verbal
configuration, devoid of human significance and cut off from the
realities of history. If this were true, however, the New Criticism would
be a threat to no one and would hardly provoke such hostility and
continued vilification. The fact is that the New Criticism is condemned
not because it treats the literary work as an empty form remote from
history and reality, but because it understands literary form in a way
that undermines the materialist ideologies pervasive among contemporary academics and intellectuals. At their best, the New Critics
stress not "mere form," but form as a structure of significance, an
embodiment of human experience. By virtue of capturing experience in a verbal form and abstracting it from the flow of time—in
other words, by creating aesthetic distance—the literary work of art
furnishes unique and invaluable access to experience via contemplation and commentary. Far from evincing a lack of interest in history and the human condition, this view of literature, in fact, strength-
ens the relation between the author and history by treating the literary work as a portal into the meaning of the ceaseless currents of
the historical process. Precisely insofar as it transcends the particular
biases and individual purposes of its author, the immediate expectations and assumptions of its original (or any other) readers, and the
political trends and socioeconomic circumstances of its era, the work
of literature is a testimony to the inherent significance and purpose

of human life.

Once we have considered the New Critics' take on form and history, the absurdity of the other common charges mentioned by Wellek becomes clear. An understanding of poetry that stresses irony and paradox hardly amounts to an emulation of the mathematical and empirical modes of scientific knowledge; rather, it urges us to recognize alternative ways of knowing that comprehend a broader spectrum of reality. Indeed, it is the New Critical vision of literature as a cognitive art that afforded this literary theory such a central place in higher education, and brings us to the last of the four allegations against the New Critics. Although it seems quixotic in our day to stigmatize any critical method that teaches students to read and write for being a mere pedagogical device, it is also true that the New Criticism, at least when it is not being abused, confers far more than a repertoire of techniques for verbal analysis. In regarding the literary work of art as a subsistent structure of meaning—that is, in granting it, in some sense, an independent ontological status—the New Criticism establishes the study of literature as a principal means of handing on the culture of Western civilization. This is an educational feat of critical importance, and it is crucially involved with the campaign mounted against the New Criticism in the course of the past several decades.

It is precisely the preoccupation with the meaning of the literary work that draws the opprobrium of postmodernist theory. At the beginning of the 1980s, Jonathan Culler fulminated against "the hegemony of New Criticism," which persists "despite the many attacks on it, despite the lack of an organized and systematic defense." This state of affairs, he maintains, is deplorable because "the most important and insidious legacy of the New Criticism is the widespread and unquestioning acceptance of the notion that the critic's job is to interpret literary works."[9] Culler proffers a list of alternative tasks for criticism:

> We have no convincing account of the role or function of
> literature in society or social consciousness. We have only
> fragmentary or anecdotal histories of literature as an insti-
> tution: we need a fuller exploration of its relation to other
> forms of discourse through which the world is organized
> and human activities are given meaning. We need a more
> sophisticated and apposite account of the role of literature
> in the psychological economies of both writers and readers;
> and in particular we ought to understand much more than
> we do about the effects of *fictional* discourse.[10]

The list goes on, but the point ought to be evident. While
traditional humanist scholars, especially literary critics, saw themselves as being engaged in a dialogue with a work of human
intellect and imagination, postmodernist academics shed the traditional reverent attitude of the humanities in their hunger for the
clinical indifference of the "human sciences." Literature as an
"institution" is to be regarded, along with "other forms of discourse," as a phenomenon; works of literature are to be treated less
as masterpieces than as specimens. "Human activities," including
literature, have no inherent meaning; meaning is rather "given" in
some arbitrary fashion through the systems or codes of the "institution," which is itself a construct, not a feature of human nature.
In denying that literary works are "autonomous artifacts" because
"they participate in a variety of systems,"[11] Culler implicitly reduces
them to the status of anthills or beehives. A poem is to be analyzed
not as a work of rational free will, but as a chemical reaction or any
other natural phenomenon. When quasi-scientific analysis is thus
substituted for interpretation, liberty is drained out of the chief
object of study in liberal education.

William Cain's discussion of the New Criticism is even more impatient than Culler's, and it is based on the same disdain for the preeminence of the close reading of individual literary works. Cain's frustration is amplified by his realization that the success of the New Criticism was based on its efficacy as an educational tool: "In one of their most intelligent strokes, the New Critics devoted themselves not only to the reform of criticism, but also to the reform of pedagogy. Their methods were—and they remain—'teachable', more so than any other method yet devised."[12] Writing in the early 1980s, Cain shrewdly observed that the real revolution had not yet occurred:

> What we have is a curious phenomenon. The New Criticism appears powerless, lacking in supporters, declining, dead or on the verge of being so. No one speaks on behalf of the New Criticism as such today, and it mostly figures in critical discourse as the embodiment of foolish ideas and misconceived techniques. But the truth is that the New Criticism survives and is prospering, and it seems to be powerless only because its power is so pervasive that we are ordinarily not even aware of it. So deeply ingrained in English studies are New Critical attitudes, values, and emphases that we do not even perceive them as the legacy of a particular movement. On the contrary: we feel them to be the natural and definitive conditions for criticism in general. It is not simply that the New Criticism has become institutionalized, but that it has gained acceptance as the institution itself. It has been transformed into "criticism," the essence of what we do as teachers and critics, the ground or given upon which everything else is based.[13]

Cain is mystified and frustrated by this state of affairs: a small band of professors from mainly Southern universities and colleges—that is, in the most impoverished and culturally isolated region of the United States—succeeds within a generation in transforming the study of literature in American higher education and, indeed, throughout the world. This New Criticism is then subjected to more than two decades of scathing and relentless ridicule, and yet, when Cain writes, it remains "institutionalized" in the scholarly practice and the curricula of English departments around the world. The one explanation that seems never to occur to him is that the New Criticism in some measure is "the essence of what we do as teachers and critics," that careful interpretation of works of demonstrable literary excellence necessarily lies at the heart of literary study.

The validity of this proposition is indicated by the decline of literary study over the ensuing fifteen years since Cain called for the disestablishment of the New Criticism in university English departments. His complaint was essentially an allegation of "formalism" without actually using the word: "We read texts, poems in particular, because we feel that they are far better, richer, more deeply textured and organically unified than any world that we know from daily experience. Returning to the text means, in this sense, turning away from the world and dwelling within the verbal structures that literature provides."[14] Literature is not enough of a subject in itself, literature professors must turn to the "world"; and involvement with the world means involvement with other disciplines, especially history and the social sciences: "To affirm that literature must be studied in its historical richness, its relevance to the present, and its relation to modern society is not to weaken or disfigure the integrity of criticism. It is, rather, a sign of our confidence in the power of literature and criticism that we feel able to teach and write 'critically' in other ways and through other disciplines."[15]

This is a plausible claim as long as one neglects to think about it. Consider the analogy of medicine: physicians *as physicians* have a far greater and more beneficent influence upon the "world" by maintaining the disciplinary integrity of their practice than by allowing medical judgments to become distorted by social or political considerations. The AIDS epidemic furnishes a discouraging negative exemplum. The obvious public health approach to an epidemic caused, overwhelmingly, by dubious and preventable human behavior (promiscuous sexual activity and intravenous drug use) would be to discourage the behavior and, when necessary, quarantine the carriers of the virus. Instead, strictly medical judgment has been clouded by widespread radical sympathy with "transgressive lifestyles," and governmental agencies have been encouraged to distribute condoms and clean syringes, measures of questionable value that implicitly condone the activities that transmit the disease. Try to imagine the American Cancer Society recommending that smokers buy filter-tip cigarettes, and that social workers distribute cigarette-holders to adolescents who *may* begin smoking.

William Cain's recommendations for reforming literary criticism and literary education amount to a similar corruption of a particular discipline by the kind of leftwing social agenda that has since been described as "politically correct." In his "Conclusion" he maintains that literary excellence is irrelevant to literary criticism and education: "[T]he question is not whether the canonical texts are 'great' (though one could quarrel in particular cases) and should be 'read' with care but is whether we should base our teaching on them and go on identifying English studies with their explication."[16] He suggests that *Uncle Tom's Cabin*, although it is deplorable as literature, should play quite as substantial a role in the curricula of American literature as *Moby Dick*, a work whose institutional status, he implies, is owing to an arbitrary set of critical norms. He offers as a central work of American literature the autobiography of Booker T. Washington, notwithstanding its flaws: "*Up from Slavery* is written in a flat, prosaic style; it is rough-hewn, awkward, rambling, anecdotal, and loosely organized."[17] Now it is certainly true that Washington's autobiography is an important work—historically, politically, socially— and it is not inconceivable that it might reasonably be studied in a course in American literature. To make such a work the foundation of a curriculum, however, is to study history, politics, or sociology rather than literature. Both *Uncle Tom's Cabin* and *Up from Slavery* have exerted more immediate force on society as a whole than *Moby Dick*, but Melville's novel is not competing in the political arena. Its influence is more subtle, more profound, and more lasting because it operates aesthetically; that is, it touches individuals in the intimate reaches of their moral and spiritual being by leading them to meditate on what it means to be human. The ultimate purpose of academic literary study is to enhance the response of students to books that confront them with ultimate questions; in the long run such questions affect the world at least as much as public policy issues.

If the methods and attitudes of the New Criticism were still pervasive when Cain first published his screed, then even he must be astonished by the speed with which his project has succeeded. In universities and colleges across the country, literature has been banished from freshman composition courses, displaced by what amounts to indoctrination in political correctness: students keep journals, work in small groups, and revise their writing endlessly in response to "peer" critiques. The topics are current events and issues shaped by writers of an almost exclusively ideological perspective. Traditional literature surveys and courses devoted to particular periods and genres and to great authors are giving way to "culture studies," which focus on marginalized groups and trendy social issues: "Emigrant Woman," "Gay Cinema," "Slave Narratives," and so on. As John Ellis points out, courses in literature in departments of

English and foreign languages are rapidly abandoning any focus on the study of literary excellence defined by specifically artistic criteria in favor of a preoccupation with a particular ideological agenda: "Many now regard social activism as the major purpose of literary criticism, and social activism of a very specific kind: the primary issue in all literary texts is the question of oppression by virtue of race, gender, and class. They view the very idea of a canon of great works as an elitist notion and even question whether there should be a distinction between literature and other kinds of writing; that, too, is elitism."[18]

The educational results have been uniformly catastrophic, but, although there is indisputable evidence of a general decline in the academic standards of colleges and universities and in the performance of students, the usual response of administrators and the most vocal segment of faculties has been to deny the gravity of the news and to shoot the messenger. The rancor that has greeted the work of Allan Bloom and E. D. Hirsch and the activities of organizations like the National Association of Scholars is typical: although neither Bloom, nor Hirsch, nor the membership of the NAS can be characterized as "conservative" in any conventional political sense, they have been condemned as "elitist" and "reactionary," and opprobrious terms like "racist," "sexist," and "homophobic" have been hurled at them.[19] Increasingly, radical academics will unblushingly assert that there is no educational crisis, because traditional norms of knowledge and skill should enjoy no particular privilege, and because one set of cultural conventions is as good as another. Linda Hutcheon provides a telling example:

> To argue, as I have been, that the reason why irony is "universally accessible"…might have less to do with interpreter competence than with the need for shared discursive con-

text, is to shift the terms of the discussion away from notions of elitism toward an acceptance of the fact that *everyone* has different knowledges and belongs to (many) different discursive communities. I personally find this a healthy corrective to the loud lamentations of the late 1980s that young people were losing what was claimed to be some sort of homogeneous, general cultural knowledge.... My own sense, right or wrong, is that they simply have *different* cultural knowledge, and that their communities' ironies are as often incomprehensible to me as mine (or Swift's) are to them.[20]

Presumably Hutcheon sees no difference in worth between *Gulliver's Travels* and *Wayne's World*, between the *Coronation Mass* and the latest CD by Crash-Test Dummies. These are all just different forms of "cultural knowledge," and there is nothing anomalous in the notion that idle, self-indulgent adolescents should set up (with a great deal of aid and encouragement from unscrupulous commercial interests) their own "culture" in opposition to the accumulated wisdom of centuries of Western Civilization. It is no wonder, then, that the New Criticism has become anathema to the regnant ideology of the contemporary university: the central goal of New Critical pedagogy was to instill in students the habit of critical discrimination—an abiding sense of the distinction between what is witty, profound, and meaningful, and what is shallow, fraudulent, and cheap. The New Criticism insisted that the experience of reading, say, a Faulkner novel was inherently superior to smoking a joint and watching a Madonna video, not in spite of but *because of* the intellectual and moral effort required.

It is important to recognize the ideological inclinations that make precisely these virtues of the New Criticism—its commitment to intellectual and artistic excellence, its insistence on the vigorous life of the mind—anathema, because it is such ideological prejudice that is the root of our current academic disaster. Although the language and tone of the current university setting are broadly Marxist, it is perhaps most helpful to conceive the radical predilections of the modern world according to the Gnostic paradigm formulated by Eric Voegelin.[21] Gnostic dualism both despises the material creation and sees it as decisive in forming the character and conduct of human beings: the evil that men do is not attributable to the sinful will of the individual; it is rather an intrinsic and hence inevitable result of physical existence. This aspect of Gnostic belief is reported not only by its ancient Catholic enemies, like St. Augustine, but also by sympathetic contemporary commentators, like Elaine Pagels.[22] At the same time, the Gnostics also believe that those who attain to a special knowledge or *gnosis* become part of an elite group who rise above the condition and destiny of ordinary mortals. Combine this with empirical science and technology, and the result looks very much like modern Marxism: the entirety of human reality, including the "superstructure" of culture and society, derives from the material forces and conditions of the economic "infrastructure." Individual human beings and all their relations with their fellow creatures are thus products of physical causation—as in the mythology of Gnosticism, with its wicked creator demiurge, the material world is an essentially evil place where the lives of human beings are reduced to a condition of miserable servitude to the necessities of physical existence.[23] Yet again there is the elite, now comprising radical intellectuals and politicians, able somehow to escape the fateful determinism of material life and, in the wake of the industrial revolution, forge a utopia in which all aspirations are realized, all desires gratified.

Obviously, only a small minority of contemporary academics would expressly subscribe to an overt Marxism, and few of my acquaintance could even identify Gnosticism with confidence; nevertheless, a set of analogous attitudes permeates a broad range of the academic community, and the influence of Marxism and associated ideologies has become especially notable among literature faculties in recent years. As John Ellis observes, Fredric Jameson, an apologist for Mao and Stalin, is "arguably the most influential of all American literary critics." The worldwide embarrassment of Marxism as a political option seems to have had no effect at all:

> The considerable vogue of Jameson's writings compels us to confront an exceedingly strange fact: just at the time when in the real world Marxism was collapsing so completely that its viability as a political theory seemed almost at an end, its influence in the universities of the English-speaking world was increasing just as dramatically.[24]

This influence is evident in a pervasive malaise in the academy—a discontent with the limits embedded in the actual nature of the human condition—and with concomitant, if contradictory, preoccupation with autonomy of the individual and the exaltation of his subjective longings. The literary critic in this frame of mind will be inclined to approach a story or a poem or a play less as an imaginative rendering or revelation of the structure of reality than as an open-ended vehicle for the free play of individual fantasies.

Now it is not hard to see why the New Criticism, with its insistence on the objective integrity of the literary work, would represent an affront to the contemporary academic ideologue. At its inception the New Criticism was, among other things, a reaction against the impressionistic "appreciations" of literature by genteel literary dabblers, against the late Romantic worship of the author as prophet or genius, and against a school of literary history that buried individual works under a mass of trivial details about influence and fashions while usually eschewing the serious task of critical judgment. The New Criticism was, above all, an assertion that a piece of fiction or poetry or drama could matter, could have significance in and of itself.

Such a view of the literary work entails certain metaphysical and moral premises incompatible with the radicalism that now dominates academic and intellectual life.[25] First, the New Criticism implies a denial of materialism, of the view that the physical realm of empirical phenomena exhausts the whole of reality. Almost all of the New Critics insist that the proper end of literary study is the work itself conceived as an independent object, and that investigations of the author's biography, of the historical situation in which he wrote, of the work's "reception history" and relations to other works of literature—all of this is ancillary to the interpretation and evaluation of the work itself.[26] These premises assume that a literary work exists independently of any particular copy or all of them collectively (the work itself is not constituted by ink and paper in the way that a painting as such consists of canvas and pigment), of the interests and purposes (conscious or unconscious) of the author, or of the responses to or experience of the work on the part of any particular reader or collection of readers in any given time or place.[27] A work of literature, then, stands as a testimony to the independence of the human spirit from material necessity: a man who can create in words a structure of significance that transcends the constraints of physical causation, or who can respond to it with sympathy and understanding, is himself by that measure a transcendent being; that is, he is a free, rational agent. By the same token, the work of literature in some ways rehabilitates that very material universe: it is seen neither as the realm of sheer darkness and despair of the ancient Gnostics nor as the meaningless grinding process of their Marxist heirs, but rather as a purposive design in which mankind is, or ought to be, temporarily at home. Literature is precisely man's imaginative ordering of his experience of the world.

The moral implications of the New Criticism are equally repugnant to the reigning academic ideologies: if a literary work is a sign of human freedom, it is also a reminder of the limits of that freedom. As a representation of reality, a literary work is a manifestation of the structure of reality that exists independently of, and sometimes in conflict with, individual expectation and desire. As an embodiment of meaning apart from author and interpreter alike, the literary work is a witness that human beings can discover significance, but not manufacture it. The New Criticism responds affirmatively to what we might call the moral realism of great literature. Consider, for example, how many tragedies manifest the dignity and grandeur of human beings as morally free agents who yet can degrade and destroy themselves through the proud abuse of freedom and a refusal to respect the limitations inherent in the nature of reality. The interpreter of drama is free to explore the richness of such a play and draw out as much as he can of its inexhaustible significance, but he must respect the integrity of the text and acknowledge its meaning as its own and not his.

It is significant that virtually every effort to discredit the New Criticism also involves an attack upon the objective integrity of the literary work of art, along with the concomitant exaltation of the reader or interpreter. Here again modern academic ideology, with its Marxist underpinnings, resembles ancient Gnosticism. "The gnostic understands Christ's message," Elaine Pagels reports, "not as offering a set of answers, but as encouragement to engage in a process of searching."[28] What is sought is not a true interpretation of the message, but a unique, wholly subjective self-realization. The authority of canonical scripture and the apostolic tradition are set aside in favor of the individual's interior divinity. "Many gnostics, then, would have agreed in principle with Ludwig Feuerbach, the nine-

teenth-century psychologist, that 'theology is really anthropology,'"
Pagels remarks, and she adds, "The gnostic movement shared certain
affinities with contemporary methods of exploring the self through
psychotherapeutic techniques."[29] Gnosticism provides a useful model
because the ancient Gnostic, like the modern Marxist, is preoccupied with escaping or transforming an unsatisfactory reality in the
interests of personal domination or self-satisfaction. Because of its
fictionality, literature can be regarded as an apt vehicle, but only if it
is severed from reality by the denial of its status as a representation
and rendered malleable to the will of the interpreter.

The various debates between the New Critics and the traditional literary historians and between the New Critics and the Chicago
Aristotelians back in the 1940s and '50s tended to be either personal
or technical—matters of tone and temperament or emphasis and
degree. In principle they were nearly all resolvable. Beginning with
the "archetypal" criticism of Northrop Frye, however, many attacks
upon the New Criticism grew out of a fundamentally incompatible
understanding of the nature and purpose of literature. Frye endeavors to reduce all works of literature to a collection of variations on
a few basic myths, universal in a vaguely Jungian sense, and he
deprecates value judgments and hierarchical discriminations deriv-
ing from aesthetic considerations. After all, if what is distinctive about
a work of literature is its embodiment of an archetypal myth, then
its unique features as a specific work will hardly be prized. From
Frye's quasi-religious perspective literature is a kind of secular scripture, with its authority drawn not from its own inherent revelatory
features, but rather conferred by the interpreter, for whom each work
serves as a vehicle for his own mythic fantasies and wish-fulfillments.[30]

In the four following decades, numerous literary theorists, however ferocious their mutual hostility, share a disdain for the integrity
of the literary work so cherished by the common enemy, the New

Critics. It turns out that the New Criticism is an ideological enemy because literature as such—imaginative literature: poetry, fiction, drama—is an ideological enemy. René Wellek quotes Roland Barthes asserting that "literature is constitutionally reactionary" and then, somewhat incredulously, proceeds to argue that Barthes is mistaken, that literature and literary figures have in fact often been in the vanguard of social protest and revolution.[31] One is reminded of E. D. Hirsch's frustrated astonishment at radical demands for the dismantling of traditional humanist disciplines in education. Surely everyone must recognize, Hirsch maintains, that it is only by mastering the verbal skills and traditional knowledge that are required by civilized literacy that one will be able to effect social changes and do away with injustice.[32]

The exasperation of Wellek and Hirsch as well as many others is understandable, but it mistakenly assumes that today's academic radicals are interested in reforming Western society and its cultural institutions when, in fact, they are mainly interested in obliterating them. Wellek himself points out that a leveling nihilism is at the heart of the matter: "All these objections to the concept of literature have one trait in common: they do not recognize quality as a criterion of literature; quality that may be either aesthetic or intellectual, but which in either case sets off a specific realm of verbal expression from daily transactions in language."[33] From the perspective of the ideologues who currently dominate the literature departments of universities, literature *is* a conservative force because it implies a standard of discrimination and judgment. Literature affronts Marxist materialism insofar as it lays claim to a transcendence of physical causes and conditions; insofar as it thus exists apart from the mind and will of any interpreter literature is an affront to Gnostic elitism—a limit on the will to appropriate the power of the word.

The New Critics regarded the study of genuine works of imagi-

native literature as a powerful civilizing force because it is educative
in the strict sense: it is a means of *leading* the student *out* of the narrow,
self-interested realm of individual ego and of the blinding constraints
of what we now call the "peer group," but which Plato called "the
Cave."[34] It is a confrontation with landmarks of cultural tradition
whose significance and authority persist from generation to generation and provide norms of thought, feeling, and behavior. In the
New Critical scheme the work of critics and scholars is ancillary to
the masterpieces that constitute literary culture. Their task is to define
and identify literary excellence and through interpretation to point
out how literature represents and reveals the nature of reality.

Now it is precisely for its high regard for literary quality that the
New Criticism is currently disdained. As Heather Dubrow and
Richard Strier, editors of a collection of New Historicist essays, aver
in their introduction, "New Criticism distinguished and privileged
'literary' language; the characteristic richness and ambiguity with
which literature was associated was [sic] seen to render it a far fitter
object of study than other types of texts, such as descriptions of cities
or political tracts." Now we know better: "...today scholars of the
English Renaissance are intensely concerned with the connections
between literary texts and social and historical phenomena—and,
indeed, with collapsing the boundaries suggested by those very distinctions."[35] In other words, the distinction between works of literature and what used to be called historical documents, while it cannot
be denied without altogether sacrificing intelligibility, is deprecated;
whatever is written is a "text," and all texts are equal. The same strictures apply to discriminations among different levels of fiction: no
distinction is allowed between serious literature of aesthetic merit,
or at least pretension, and what once would have been called sub-
literature, pulp fiction, or *Kitsch*. Occasionally an especially egre-
gious example surfaces in the newspapers—the doctoral disserta-

tion on Madonna comes to mind—but "scholarship" dealing with "popular culture" is a growth industry; and, in addition to the countless explicit examples, the mentality of popularization has infected the study of traditional parts of the curriculum. Perhaps the most revealing indicator of the situation is the number of college professors who seem to spend more time listening to hard rock and watching MTV than reading poetry.

There are two main consequences of all this: the reduction of literature to the material of sophistry—so much grist for the ideological mill—and the concomitant exaltation of the critic or interpreter, who takes precedence over the putative object of his inquiries. Frank Lentricchia maintains that the effort to interpret a text objectively is merely a form of collaboration with the political status quo, since "Literature is inherently nothing; or it is a body of rhetorical strategies waiting to be seized."[36] His former Duke colleague, Stanley Fish, argues that when the interpreter approaches a literary text not with the aim of *demonstrating* its meaning and value, but rather of *persuading* his audience to accept it on his terms, then the interpreter supersedes the text:

> But perhaps the greatest gain that falls to us under a persuasion model is a greatly enhanced sense of the importance of our activities. (In certain quarters of course, where the critical ideal is one of self-effacement, this will be perceived to be the greatest danger.) No longer is the critic the humble servant of texts whose glories exist independently of anything he might do; it is what he does, within the constraints embedded in the literary institution, that brings texts into being and makes them available for analysis and appreciation. The practice of literary criticism is not something one must apologize for; it is absolutely essential not only to the

maintenance of, but to the very production of, the objects of its attention.[37]

In the formulations of both Lentricchia and Fish, the critic does not seek to elucidate the vision of reality represented by a work of literature, but instead sets out to bend a "text"—so much plastic verbiage—to his own version of things, and to manipulate an audience in the process. Of course, as Fish's language reveals, this interpretive license only operates "within the constraints embedded in the literary institution," or, as he usually calls it, the "interpretive community." It turns out that maximum freedom is maximum bondage, and the critic is as much a product of his socioeconomic situation as the "text" he interprets.

This state of affairs was anticipated by Cleanth Brooks fifty years ago. In the preface to *The Well Wrought Urn*, perhaps the single most important book of the New Criticism, he observed, "The temper of our times is strongly relativistic." In the face of this relativism, Brooks asserts the propriety, indeed the necessity, of seeing "what residuum, if any, is left after we have referred the poem to its cultural matrix." He explicitly affirms the importance of literary history, and anyone familiar with Brooks's own critical practice will be aware of his profound knowledge of the historical context of the literary works he treats. "Yet," he continues, "if poetry exists as poetry in any meaningful sense, the attempt must be made [to view it *sub specie aeternitatis*]. Otherwise the poetry of the past becomes significant merely as cultural anthropology, and the poetry of the present, merely as a political, or religious, or moral instrument."[38] The state of affairs about which Brooks offers this caution a half-century ago is now cheerfully flaunted as the New Historicism.

It is the first chapter of *The Well Wrought Urn*, "The Language of Paradox," which most vividly reveals the implications of the New Criticism and of the ideological theories that have arisen to challenge it—not only because of the intrinsic interest of the chapter, but also because it has been singled out for a demonstration of "deconstruction" by Jonathan Culler. In this chapter Brooks sets out to show that the language of poetry is inherently paradoxical, a blend of "irony and wonder"; that is, what distinguishes a genuine poem is that its verbal pattern, especially its various figures of speech, cannot be reduced to any set of plain prose statements; or at least that any such paraphrase is not the same as or convertible with the poem. In the language of economics, poetry is not fungible. It is precisely this irreducibility that constitutes a poem's independent existence.

The poem that Brooks adduces to illustrate this view is "The Canonization" by John Donne, a brilliant, if extravagant and sometimes risqué, deployment of religious language in defense of human sexual love. The poem is by turns outrageously and defiantly witty, tender, and impassioned. What is more, there are numerous features of the poem that seem to reflect Donne's own life—he destroyed his hopes for preferment at Court and fell into disgrace and financial ruin by eloping with a very young woman living in his employer's household. The poem, however, was not published until after the poet's death, and its actual relation to events in his life remains a matter of speculation. Brooks's central thesis is that the seemingly contradictory tensions in "The Canonization"—the ironic, even bawdy references to sexual intercourse jostling against the assertions of human love's transcendence—finally converge in a unified vision of our experience of love, which cannot be expressed in our ordinary, common-sense statements about it. The vision that is verbally manifest in the poem may or may not have been inspired or provoked by this or that incident or preoccupation in the life of the man John Donne, but the poem itself is distinct from the aims and experiences of the poet, and accessible to the experience of readers in the way that the lived experiences of another is not.

Consider, for example, the central stanza of "The Canonization":

Call us what you will, wee are made such by love;
  Call her one, mee another flye,
We'are Tapers too, and at our owne cost die,
  And wee in us finde the'Eagle and the Dove.
    The Phoenix ridle hath more wit
    By us, we two being one, are it.
So, to one neutrall thing both sexes fit,
  Wee dye and rise the same, and prove
  Mysterious by this love.[39]   (19-27)

There are more puzzles and obscurities and complex tonal layers than I can begin to unravel here (that, after all, is the point), but I do wish to call attention to the closing couplet. Christ's Resurrection from death, one of the *mysteries* of the Christian faith, is evoked here at the same time *and in the same words* as a bawdy Renaissance pun on "dying" as the attainment of sexual climax. One could choose to regard this as mere blasphemy, but the tone of the poem as a whole seems to preclude such a simplification, though the lines do gain much of their force from the *suggestion* of blasphemy. This passage, and finally the poem as a whole, sets out to acknowledge and, so far as possible, to embrace our entire equivocal experience of human sexuality, which is funny, embarrassing, obscene, "dirty"; exciting and pleasurable and yet repugnant; tender, exalted, sacred. Marriage, we must remember, is regarded by some Christian communions as a sacrament and by all as a holy and honorable estate, and it is consummated by sexual intercourse. Brooks's comment on the quoted lines is instructive: "The lovers after the act are the same. Their love is not exhausted in mere lust. This is their title to canonization. Their love is like the phoenix.... Most important of all, the sexual meaning of 'die' does not contradict the other meanings."[40]

It is not my purpose here to defend every aspect of Brooks's reading of "The Canonization" (I myself find the poem less solemn and more boisterous than he); what is at stake, however, is his view of this poem—of any effective poem—as a triumph over the inadequacies of our ordinary language. Samuel R. Levin, a theorist of metaphor, draws attention to "our awareness of the poet's struggle against the limitations inherent in the capacities of human language."[41] The heart of the New Critical account of poetry, of literature in general, is the discovery of how the work of imaginative writers pushes back those limitations, yet at the same time, in the very act of challenging them, reminds us of the ineluctable presence of limitations by the extraordinary literary devices required for the confrontation.

The enemies to whom Brooks and his generation were accustomed were likely to attack from the direction of positivism or a quasi-scientific rationalism: literature was dismissed as merely "emotive," inaccurate, not "empirically verifiable." Hence the New Critics were at pains to stress that the language of imaginative literature and of literary criticism was, in its own way, as precise as the language of science: although the knowledge embodied in literature lacked the mathematical certitude of physics, it was, even so, objective in its own fashion. From the deconstructionist perspective, however, no discourse can boast precision or objectivity; no signifier can make the signified fully present or available to the mind. Everything, then, is "literature," but this is not an honorific term. Scientific and philosophic discourse, legal documents, and pastoral elegies are all chains of signifiers that never terminate in the signified: textuality is our prison from which there is no escape.

The typical procedure of deconstruction is to grasp a loose thread in the textual weave of a discourse and to proceed with the unraveling. Jonathan Culler seizes upon Brooks's comment on the fourth stanza of "The Canonization," where the "sonnets" and "hymnes" celebrating the passion of the lovers are compared to a "well wrought urne." "The poem is an instance of the doctrine which it asserts," Brooks says; "it is both the assertion and the realization of the assertion. The poet has actually before our eyes built within the song the 'pretty room' with which he says the lovers can be content. The poem itself is the well-wrought urn which can hold the lovers' ashes and which will not suffer in comparison with the prince's 'halfe-acre tombe.'"[42] According to Jonathan Culler, Brooks is attributing to the poem a "self-reference"—a "self-reflexivity...seen as self-knowledge, self-possession, or a self-understanding or presence of the poem to itself." But, he assures us, "Under exegetical pressure, self-reference demonstrates the impossibility of self-possession." Culler proceeds to insist that "The Canonization" is "not so much a self-contained urn as a chain of discourses and representations"; for "if the poem is the urn, then one of the principal features of the urn is that it portrays people responding to the urn." It turns out that Cleanth Brooks himself becomes part of the poem "he thought he was analyzing from the outside":

> This self-referential element in Donne's poem does not produce or induce closure in which the poem harmoniously is the thing it describes. In celebrating itself as urn the poem incorporates a celebration of the urn and thus becomes something other than the urn; and if the urn is taken to include the response to the urn, then the responses it anticipates, such as Brooks's, become a part of it and prevent it from closing. Self-reference does not close it in upon itself but leads to a proliferation of representations, a series of invocations and urns, including Brooks's *The Well Wrought Urn*.[43]

Now there are two important points to notice here. First, "self-referentiality" is neither Brooks's term nor his concept; Culler imposes it without justification on his predecessor's discussion. For a poem to be "both the assertion and the realization of the assertion" does not entail "self-reference" or "self-reflexivity." "The Canonization" refers not to itself, but to what it represents: the speech of a fictive character, whose attitudes and ideas doubtless had their origin in the consciousness of John Donne, but who is certainly not identical with that poet. (The *speaker* or *persona* is as "present" as he ever was; the actual man John Donne is long since dead.) Indeed, the very notion of referentiality is suspect, or at least problematic, with respect to poetry and other works of literature. In strict terms, the reference of a word or of an entire discourse is its designation of a particular object, event, place, or concept in the real world. Imaginative literature does not properly *refer* in a factually accurate sense, or if it does, accuracy of reference is not relevant to its status as literature, as a fictional representation. "What childe is there," writes Sir Philip Sidney, "that, comming to a Play, and seeing *Thebes* written in great Letters vpon an olde doore, doth beleeue that it is *Thebes*? If then a man can ariue, at that childes age, to know that the Poets persons and dooings are but pictures what should be, and not stories what haue beene, they will neuer giue that lye to things not affirmatiuely but allegorically and figuratiuelie written."[44] "The Canonization" is a discourse duplicated in numerous copies in various kinds of documents that actually exist in the world, but it *refers* to nothing: it is a dramatic *representation* of an utterance by a fictional character. The irrelevance of referentiality to poetry becomes paradoxically clearer in a poem that makes specific, identifiable references. The first, shorter version of Alexander Pope's *The Dunciad* ridicules Lewis Theobalds as the King of Dunces. The second, longer version replaces Theobalds with the Whig poetaster Colley Cibber. The later version is the richer, more powerful poem, but not because

Cibber is a more appropriate target than Theobalds. Pope and his friend and contemporary Jonathan Swift are great satirists because their works are still effective and profound long after the individuals and incidents that provoked them have been forgotten. It is probably true that most writers are moved to write by particular events or individuals: a work of literature is precisely a piece of writing that transcends its occasion. Culler has misunderstood Brooks and, worse yet, misunderstood the nature of literature.

The second notable flaw in Culler's critique is similar: when Brooks says, "The poem itself is the well wrought urn," this is a statement of a different order than, say, "The poem comprises forty-five lines." Brooks uses "well wrought urn" metaphorically, much as Donne does; and so the urn was "something other than an urn" long before Culler noticed. He may as well require Brooks to produce an enameled clay vessel decorated with "Countries, Townes, Courts"; or Keats to account for the deserted village on his "Grecian Urn." The language of criticism is not the same as the language of poetry, but it is also not the language of the exact sciences. Often an explication works by taking the poet's metaphors and looking at them from varying angles. To literalize an interpreter's metaphors is either bad faith or foolishness. For more than two decades now, the deconstructionists have been quite the cleverest denizens of English departments, but occasionally they resemble the dullest undergraduates in their inability to distinguish between figurative and literal language—or between poetry and pottery.

To be sure, a major goal of the deconstructive "project," which it has bequeathed to postmodernism generally, is to put in question such binary oppositions as literal/figurative and literary/scientific; however, as the example of Jonathan Culler shows, we usually get question-begging rather than argument. His deconstruction of Brooks's reading of "The Canonization" begins by *assuming* that the notion of self-referentiality applies to a poem in the same fashion as it applies to, say, a legal document that defines itself. Likewise, he assumes that the nature of signification renders nugatory any real distinction between fact and fiction, between literal statement and metaphor. Of course these are the very points that the deconstructionist is supposed to prove. But in fact deconstruction can, finally, prove nothing, for by denying the efficacy of discourse it undermines the significance of proof. Deconstruction is typical of much contemporary theory in hating the Word as an embodiment or manifestation of truth. This negation at the heart of deconstruction is an essential element of all the current critical approaches that brandish the term "postmodern." The integrity of the fictive world of imaginative literature is thus under attack because literature defines itself in terms of the truth which it is not, but which it represents.

A poem cannot exhaust reality, but it can arrest it: it manifests a vision of experience available in no other way. This is only possible because, like a physical urn, it is a distinct substantial object: only by its difference from human experience can a poem represent that experience, even as the urn can be a metaphor for a poem only if it is not itself a poem. The alternative to "crystalline closure" is not, then, an endless and chaotic "repetition and proliferation,"[45] but a structured relationship of significance. Literature helps us to know life precisely in the fashion that postmodernists deny: literature dramatizes experience by establishing a vantage point *outside* it. It is precisely because "The Canonization" occupies a different existential space from John Donne, Cleanth Brooks, and flesh-and-blood love affairs that we are able to learn so much from it about Donne, Brooks, and love—and about ourselves.

CHAPTER TWO

Derrida or Deity?
Deconstruction in the
Presence of the Word

I t is commonly asserted that deconstruction is finished as the dominant theoretical perspective of the postmodernist literary scene, that it has been displaced by the New Historicism, a movement of American origin, or its mainly British alter ego, "cultural poetics." In a superficial sense this proposition is true, but it requires substantial qualification. As Stanley Fish points out, "if there is now no vigorous discussion of deconstruction in the academy, it is because its lessons have been absorbed and its formulations—the irreducibility of difference, the priority of the signifier over the signified, the social construction of the self—have been canonized; and if poststructuralism has given way to postmodernism as the new all-purpose term, it is because the implications of the first term are now being extended far beyond the realm of aesthetics and philosophy to the very texture of everyday life."[1] Deconstruction, then, has seized the role formerly assumed by the New Criticism at the heart of the scholarly and pedagogical activities of academic literary study. Until quite recently professors of literature in American universities, both in their publications and their classrooms, were fundamentally engaged in the explication and

interpretation of literary works and the assessment of their significance in literary history. Thus scholars and their students were
principally concerned with discovering and understanding meaning. Under the pervasive influence of deconstruction, this basic task
is rapidly giving way to the dismantling of meaning and the neglect
of understanding in the interest of will: while the chief aim of the
New Criticism was interpretation, deconstruction sets out from the
assumption that there are only misinterpretations of greater or
lesser force or utility.

Pursued to its logical conclusion of illogicality—of nihilistic
chaos—deconstruction will only succeed in canceling itself out along
with everything else; however, postmodernists have learned to live
with cognitive dissonance and apply the solvent of deconstruction
only to the ideas of their perceived enemies. Henry Louis Gates, Jr.,
furnishes an ingenuously blatant example:

> The classic critique of our attempts to reconstitute our own
> subjectivity, as women, as blacks, etc., is that of Jacques
> Derrida: "This is the risk. The effect of Law is to build a
> structure of the subject, and as soon as you say, 'well, the
> woman is a subject and this subject deserves equal rights,'
> and so on—then you are caught in the logic of
> phallocentricism and you have rebuilt the empire of Law."
> To expressions such as this, made by a critic whose stands
> on sexism and racism have been exemplary, we must respond
> that the Western male subject has long been constituted
> historically for himself and in himself. And, while we readily
> accept, acknowledge, and partake of the critique of *this*
> subject as transcendent, to deny us the process of exploring
> and reclaiming our subjectivity before we critique it is the
> critical version of the grandfather clause, the double privi-
> leging of categories that happen to be *preconstituted*.[2]

Such is the impeccable logic of deconstructive illogic: the idea of Western Civilization is hollow because deconstruction shows that all conceptions are self-contradictory; but since the concept of deconstruction is itself contradictory, it can be happily ignored when its implications prove inconvenient for our own favorite ideals. Although deconstruction has lost some of its prominence and luster in the academic world, it remains, as Fish intimates, indispensable for the flourishing of postmodernism. There is irony here, insofar as deconstruction reveals the emptiness of the postmodern "project," even while making it possible.

The method of interpretation—or of (mis)interpretation, as its proponents might write it—developed by Jacques Derrida and purveyed among American literary scholars by Paul de Man has been controversial and deliberately confrontational from the first. Dissenters have accused deconstruction of subverting objective standards of literary explication and evaluation, of blurring the distinction between criticism and imaginative literature, of deprecating the author and authorial intention for the sake of the tangential gambits of the critical reader, and of engaging in a generally self-indulgent, irresponsible style of writing that undercuts the scholarly and educational aims of academic discourse. Exponents of deconstruction have rarely shown any inclination to dispel such charges. "Criticism is...continuous with the language of literature," writes J. Hillis Miller, and he proceeds in much the same vein:

> The poem [Shelley's *The Triumph of Life*], like all texts, is "unreadable," if by "readable" one means having a single, definitive interpretation. In fact, neither the "obvious" reading nor the deconstructionist reading is "univocal." Each contains, necessarily, its enemy within itself, is itself both host and parasite. The deconstructionist reading contains the

obvious one and vice versa. Nihilism is an unalienable alien
presence within Occidental metaphysics, both in poems and
in the criticism of poems.[3]

The elliptical style of argument and the philosophical pretensions
are equally typical of deconstructionist prose and equally irritating
to an older tradition of British and American literary scholarship,
which for the past thirty years has been forced to grapple with a
theory in which more is at stake than a new reading of Shelley.
Unlike the vast majority of his American disciples who are denizens
of literature departments, Derrida's training was in philosophy;
hence he has forced academic literary critics to realize that critical
theory is inscribed within a set of metaphysical assumptions. It has
proved unsettling for old-fashioned philologists to perceive that
when the status of being itself is put in question, the possibility of
meaning is doubly problematic.

By the neologism "deconstruction" Derrida seems to mean not
only a method of radical textual analysis, but a whole new way of
thinking about the human experience of reality. What is, finally, to
be deconstructed is the whole "logocentric" tradition of Western
metaphysics, of "ontotheology" as Derrida often calls it. From a
Derridean perspective, reality itself—or at least mankind's perception of it—is a kind of writing, a signifier of an absence that can never
be grasped or realized; and deconstruction seizes on the loose linguistic threads to unravel the textuality of the world. Derrida thus
lays siege to the intellectual norms of Western culture. Yet
deconstruction is less alarming for its actual philosophical force than
for its success in demoralizing the academic world with the per-
vasiveness of its rhetoric and attitude. It is something of a paradox
that, while deconstruction is a corrosive solvent to the utopian pieties of Marxism and atheistic humanism, the principles of the

Christian faith remain untouched, although Christianity is the ultimate "ontotheology" or "philosophy of presence." While the
Derridean abyss opens sickeningly at the feet of every variety of
secularist, it offers little terror to Christians, whose saints have plumbed
its depths in centuries past.

Derrida's publications have been appearing in the English-
speaking world for more than thirty years, but the works of the late
'60s and early '70s, which established his fundamental themes, remain the most important and influential. He first drew broad attention in this country in 1966 with a paper delivered at an international symposium at Johns Hopkins University. Under the title,
"Structure, Sign, and Play in the Discourse of the Human Sciences,"
this paper was basically a critique of the structuralism of anthro-
pologist Claude Lévi-Strauss just when structuralism was enjoying
its greatest influence and prestige. The following year saw the publication of three books by Derrida, *Speech and Phenomena*, a critique
of Husserl's theory of signs, *Of Grammatology*, a critique of the Western world's traditional "privileging" of speech over writing, and
Writing and Difference, a collection of essays dealing with associated
themes. In 1972 Derrida published two more collections of essays,
Margins, which includes the definitive version of "Différance," and
Dissemination, which reprints "Plato's Pharmacy," Derrida's landmark
discussion of the treatment of writing in the *Phaedrus*. By the early
1980s all of these works, as well as others by Derrida, had been translated into English. Although he continues to produce new books,
which are quickly translated, none of the recent work seems to make
significant additions or alterations to the initial dissection of traditional Western notions of philosophy and language. Indeed, Derrida
seems to have been largely repeating himself for two decades. This
may be the appropriate fate for the propounder of a philosophy (or
a *misosophy*?) that makes such a doubtful endeavor of saying any-

thing at all, much less anything new.

A useful perspective on deconstruction is secured by approaching it as the ingrate stepchild of Parisian structuralism, an academic movement that sought to place the "human sciences" on the same epistemological footing as the physical sciences. The principal intellectual inspiration for structuralism lies in the work of Marx and Freud, who both attempted to analyze human behavior in terms of objectively conceived economic or psychological structures without worrying about the messy, unscientific business of the conscious individual will. The methodological model for structuralism, however, came from linguistics, most notably the *Course in General Linguistics*, posthumously compiled from lecture notes by students of Ferdinand de Saussure. Hence leading structuralists have usually been linguists (like Roman Jakobson), or those who apply the structural model of linguistics to other disciplines such as psychology (like Jacques Lacan) or anthropology (like Claude Lévi-Strauss).

It has been widely noted that the key to Derrida's thought is his peculiar view that the basic principles of Saussurian linguistics— "That no intrinsic relationship obtains between the two parts of the sign, signifier and signified"—undermines even the structuralist enterprise itself. A signifier, or sound-image, Saussure maintains, is arbitrarily linked to a signified, or concept; that is, since the sounds of words, or signifiers, are unmotivated conventions, a sign is a structure of difference: "The important thing in the word is not the sound alone but phonic differences that make it possible to distinguish this word from all others, for differences carry signification."[4] From this principle of the arbitrariness of the means of signification, Derrida infers that all discourse is subject to an inevitable leakage of meaning precisely in order to mean at all. The very act of meaning—that is, of signifying—implies the absence of the thing signified, which, therefore, can be grasped not in itself but only by means of the substituted signifier. Hence we confront not merely the gap between *res* and *verbum* (thing and word), but a gap or, to use a term borrowed from rhetoric by Paul de Man, an *aporia* within the sign itself—within the complex of signified and signifier. As a result the structuralist can never stand outside the structure that he posits; he, too, is an inmate of the "prisonhouse of language."[5]

Now for Derrida this principle of linguistics has important metaphysical—I should say *anti*-metaphysical—implications. Since man inhabits a universe of discourse, he is entangled in a chain of signifiers referring to absent signifieds: the world is thus one great circular definition. Every term or concept is marked by what Derrida calls the *trace* of its incompletion and undecidability, and this stricture applies with full force to the subjective consciousness, which can only take shape within the framework of language or discourse. In his earliest published works he attacks the notion of the self-possessed intentional subject of Husserlian phenomenology. There is no pre-linguistic thought, Derrida maintains, fully present to the conscious ego—hence no self that transcends the limitations of linguistic temporality: "As soon as we admit this continuity of the now and the not-now, perception and nonperception, in the zone of primordiality common to primordial impression and retention, we admit the other into the self-identity of the *Augenblick*; nonpresence and nonevidence are admitted into the *blink of an instant*. There is duration to the blink, and it closes the eye."[6] As a result, our knowledge, deployed in temporally extended signifiers, cannot all be simultaneously present. We know only in memory or in expectation; hence we know only what is not here and not now—that is, what is not present.

Our world of consciousness is not, then, inhabited by the presentation of its intentional objects, but by *re-presentations* implicated with *différance*. This neologism, spelled with an "a" rather than an "e" in the last syllable, is derived from the French verb *différer*, which, like its Latin cognate *differo*, means both to defer in time or postpone and to differ or be spatially distinct. The arbitrary change in spelling, perceptible to the eye in writing but not to the ear in speech, highlights Derrida's preoccupation with the paradoxical priority of writing over speech insofar as the former reveals more directly the arbitrary nature of signification. The word "child," for example, is a "sound-image" that signifies a complex, equivocal notion: offspring, non-adult, immature person, innocent or inexperienced person, and so on. But then, all of these terms, these "signifieds," also turn out to be signifiers, in the sense that in each case another sound-image stands between the mind and the meaning, and they likewise ramify into another set of signifieds that spawn more signifiers. There can be no end to this process, no final, central concept or signified that can logically or fully account for the meanings that float freely around the arbitrary sound-image "child." *A fortiori* no particular visual image in the mind or in actual reality (a specific, individual child) can exhaust the implications of the term. "Child" has meaning *only* because it is distinguishable (different) from other sound-images ("wild," "mild," "man," "adult," "baby," "parent"), *not* because it is rooted in a stable signification or actually embodies in itself a particular meaning. Derrida thus seems to have gone a step beyond nominalism, which maintains that universals or concepts are mere "names," that only particular, individual entities have real, substantial existence. He seems to suggest that even the particular things lack real existence, that substance occurs only in a matrix of accidents. Derrida calls this condition *différance*.

Différance, then, is the defect or failure of completion inscribed not only in every utterance, but also in every experience; the *trace* is the token, silent and invisible—literally nonexistent—of this interval or gap in being. Because writing is so plainly representational, a "supplement" for speech, it manifests the "textuality" of human experience. Hence it is characteristically repressed in favor of the spoken word, with its illusion of unmediated presence, by the Western metaphysical tradition that ceaselessly strives to occupy the vacancy in human existence, to fill the hole in being:

> The subordination of the trace to the full presence summed up in the logos, the humbling of writing beneath a speech dreaming its plenitude, such are the gestures required by an onto-theology determining the archeological and eschatological meaning of being as presence, as parousia, as life without difference: another name for death, historical metonymy where God's name holds death in check. That is why, if this movement begins its era in the form of Platonism, it ends in infinitist metaphysics. Only infinite being can reduce the difference in presence. In that sense, the name of God, at least as it is pronounced within classical rationalism, is the name of indifference itself.[7]

Hence Derrida is fond of outraging the science of linguistics with the quixotic proposition that writing is prior to speech. All linguists, including Saussure, naturally observe that human beings spoke before they wrote, and that writing is merely a representation of real language (with its root word, *lingua*, "tongue"). Derrida's contrary point is that speech itself is a representation of ideas, which exist only in words, hence only as representations. Writing is thus "prior" as the most overtly representational means of signification.

Of course, considered as a contribution to linguistics or to intellectual history, deconstruction is sheer nonsense—an out-of-control metaphor. John Ellis has demonstrated conclusively that Derrida abuses the terms and concepts developed by Ferdinand de Saussure and generalizes irresponsibly about language in a way that not only has no basis in Saussure, but actually contradicts him. "It follows that deconstructive logic makes its way not by any genuinely logical means," Ellis complains, "but, instead, by its psychological appeal." But for all the thoroughness and lucidity of his critique, Ellis in one sense misses the point. Deconstruction is not just "illogical"; it is anti-logical, and this characteristic is precisely the source of its "psychological appeal." It seems to furnish a means of argument for those who reject not only the traditional canon of great books, but even the canons of reasoned discourse. Ellis claims that "feminists and Marxists are very mistaken to see support for their position in deconstruction's rhetoric. For they are surely attempting to identify *particular* omissions from the center and making *specific* proposals to change the consensus, which is as it should be."[8] Surely they are not. Thoroughly discredited as an economic system or political philosophy, Marxism is now no more than a fashionable costume for academic antinomianism among the pampered professors of the affluent West. Whatever the merits of the original feminist case against injustice to women, much current feminism—especially in the academic world—has degenerated into a hateful fanaticism detached from the realities of human nature and the human situation.[9]

To be sure, deconstruction has not infrequently been a source of unease among critics on the radical left. Edward W. Said, for example, questions Derrida's ideological commitment:

> If everything in a text is always equally open to suspicion and to affirmation, then the differences between one class interest and another, between oppressor and oppressed, one discourse and another, one ideology and another, are virtual in—but never crucial to making the decisions about—the finally reconciling element of textuality.[10]

The implicit charge here is that Derrida is unwilling to get his hands dirty in history and radical politics. Frank Lentricchia similarly complains, "Derrida's deconstructive project is formalist through and through."[11] It is hard to imagine a more damning term in the current critical lexicon than "formalist" (it is the epithet hurled at the New Critics), but it is little more than a stalking horse: the real worry is that Marx is quite as vulnerable to deconstruction—really more so—than Plato or Hegel. "A speech dreaming its plenitude" is a perfect description of the discourse of the radical left, with its binary oppositions of class conflict and its "eschatological" project of full human "presence" in a classless society purged of alienation and repression. Deconstructed Marxism would be a secularized millenarianism, a self-deceived, materialist logocentricism; and any privileged term or concept—"history," "gender," "diversity"—can be dismantled with equal facility. Still, in the absence of a convincing affirmative vision of their own, today's academic terrorists cannot do without deconstruction: it is their equivalent of polemical gelignite, and having a bomb go off in your face is the risk run by every saboteur.

The relationship between traditional Christianity and deconstruction is of another order. Most of Derrida's impact—his shock value—arises from his demonstration that supposedly critical philosophies, exemplars of post-Enlightenment thought, are covertly logocentric; that is, they are founded on the treatment of human reason or consciousness as self-sufficient or absolute even as they claim to deliver us from divine absolutes. As the force of God's presence is diminished, the autonomous human subject becomes the "transcendental signified" of its own signification. Derrida forcefully maintains that to establish a metaphysical system on the basis of human reason is to sneak God in through the back door, because it amounts to the deification of humanity. Christianity, however, has always been *explicitly* "logocentric" insofar as it places Christ, the incarnate Logos or "Word," at the center of reality. Thus while making the very strongest claims for the discourse of reason, the Christian's confidence is rooted in the paradoxes of faith, in a confrontation with God—the radically *other* for whom every sign is inadequate. Derrida has shown little interest in the way his own issues have been raised by Christian thinkers like St. Augustine and St. Thomas Aquinas. St. Augustine, for example, radically deconstructed the human condition sixteen centuries ago: "What is a man, any man, when only a man."[12]

In the *Confessions* Augustine's preoccupation with time and memory anticipates Derrida's notion of *différance*. Augustine recognizes that even as we cannot grasp the present moment in our temporal existence in the physical world, even so our speech is never wholly and immediately present. But Augustine maintains that these limitations are the very conditions of our being, action, and knowledge. In order for discrete substances—beings distinct from necessary Being—to exist at all, they must suffer displacement in time, and the same temporal displacement is requisite for the differential process of speech:

> So much you gave to these things, because they are parts of a whole, which do not all exist at the same time, but all function in the universe, of which they are parts, succeeding one another then giving way. Notice how our speech operates in the same way by means of signifying sounds. For an utterance is not complete, if one word does not give way, when its syllables have sounded, so that another can succeed it.[13]

Augustine perceives that in its very temporal progression, speech lacks complete reality, and, in this, it faithfully mirrors the incompleteness of human—indeed, of all temporal—existence. But the discontinuities of spatio-temporal existence are not an insufficiency of being as such. The very incompleteness of being as it unfolds in time and space entails absolute Being as its ground; the stream of our words into the abyss of oblivion—of signifiers pursuing elusive signifieds—entails the being of the immutable Word of God:

> And what was being spoken is not ended, and something else spoken, so that everything might be said, but everything is said at the same time and eternally; otherwise there would be time and change, and no true eternity or immortality.[14]

Différance, Derrida maintains, inhabits the existential gaps of time: "nonpresence and nonevidence are admitted into the *blink of the instant*. There is a duration to the blink, and it closes the eye."[15] But this is a merely human perspective. St. Augustine might reply that God does not blink; His eye never closes.

In fact, Augustine brings to bear an analogy in order to illustrate the insufficiency of language in denominating even what we as human beings know, beyond the limits of semantic specification:

> I may have said quite confidently that the Father and the Son and the Holy Spirit, of one and the same substance, God the Creator, the Almighty Trinity, function inseparably together: but it cannot thus be shown inseparably by means of a wholly unequal and especially corporeal creature. Even so the Father and the Son and the Holy Spirit cannot be named by our words, which in any case issue in material sounds, except in their own distinct and proper intervals of time, occupied by all the syllables of each word. As they are in their own substance, the three are one, the Father and the Son and the Holy Spirit, in no movement of time above every creature the very same, without any intervals or time or space, together the same from eternity unto eternity, as eternity

itself, which is not without truth and charity. In my words, however, the Father and the Son and the Holy Spirit are separated, and they cannot be spoken at the same time, and they hold divided places in visible letters. Even so when I name my memory, understanding, and will, the three names refer to three individual items, but nevertheless these particulars have been fashioned by all three faculties; for there is none of these three names which is not the work of my memory, understanding, and will together. Just so the Trinity together produces the voice of the Father, the flesh of the Son, and the dove of the Holy Spirit, even when these particulars refer to particular persons.[16]

What Augustine here suggests is that the very realization of the inadequacy of our words, provides a greater weight and credibility to the Word. Even as we are aware that our discourse cannot fully specify or comprehend the workings of our own rational souls, which produce that discourse, even so we are aware that our incapacity fully to apprehend reality does not compromise the fullness of the real.

Derrida of course demurs; he dismisses even "the most negative order of negative theology" as dependent upon the prior trace of *différance*, which "has neither existence nor essence," which "belongs to no category of being, present or absent." Like the lines that define plane surfaces in geometry while having no breadth themselves, *différance* is the negative prerequisite of any apprehension of being:

> *Différance* is not only irreducible to any ontological or theological—ontotheological—reappropriation, but as the very opening of the space in which ontotheology—philosophy— produces its system and its history, it includes ontotheology, inscribing it and exceeding it without return.[17]

But if *différance* is the all-encompassing ground of being, then this ground is a hole, an abyss, and being itself becomes problematic, endlessly "deferred":

> "Older" than Being itself, such a *différance* has no name in our language. But we "already know" that if it is unnameable, it is not provisionally so, not because our language has not yet found or received this *name*, or because we would have to seek it in another language, outside the finite system of our own. It is rather because there is no *name* for it at all, not even the name of essence or of Being, not even that of "*différance*," which is not a name, which is not a pure nominal unity, and unceasingly dislocates itself in a chain of differing and deferring substitutions.[18]

"This unnameable," Derrida continues, "is not an ineffable Being which no name could approach: God, for example"; it is rather "the play which makes possible nominal effects." For Derrida, "word" is always spelled with a lower case "w": "There is nothing kerygmatic about this 'word,' provided that one perceives its decapita(liza)tion."[19]

Derrida's reduction of metaphysics to a *mise en abîme* rests on his apprehension of the spatiotemporal dislocation of human perception and signification. Our saying and knowing are attenuated in time and space. *To be in time*, Derrida urges, is a virtual contradiction because movement in time involves continuous loss of presence: "The present alone is and ever will be. Being is presence or the modification of presence."[20] Hence even the assertion of the contrary deconstructs itself as it unfolds as temporal speech:

> The *I am*, being experienced only as an *I am present*, itself presupposes the relationship with presence in general, with

being as presence. The appearing of the *I* to itself in the *I am* is thus originally a relation with its own possible disappearance. Therefore, *I am* originally means *I am mortal. I am immortal* is an impossible proposition. We can even go further: as a linguistic statement "I am he who am" is the admission of a mortal.[21]

Derrida's appraisal of the paradox of temporal being is by no means novel; St. Augustine grapples with it at great length in the *Confessions* and reaches basically the same conclusion regarding being in time:

> Those two times, therefore, past and present, how can they be, when the past already is not, and the future is not yet? As for the present, if it were always present and did not cross over into the past, it would not be time but rather eternity. If then the present comes to be as time only because it moves into the past, how can we say *it is*, when the cause of its being is that it will not be; in fact, how can we say truly that time is, except insofar as it tends not to be?[22]

What distinguishes this passage from Derrida's disquisition on "temporalization" is that Augustine invokes the concept of eternity, which Derrida steadfastly ignores. For the latter, the lurking (non)presence of the trace, of *différance*—the fissure in being—undermines the possibility of *simplicity*, which is a necessary attribute of Eternity, of God. But Derrida's view fails to take into account his own insights regarding the fallibility of man's knowledge. "There never was any 'perception,'" he writes, and "contrary to what our desire cannot fail to be tempted into believing, the thing itself always escapes."[23] But what "always escapes" cannot be confidently relegated to nonexistence. Derrida succeeds in refuting the transcendental aspirations of man *qua* man, as temporal creature: Kant's own logic is turned relentlessly against him, and the Kantian subject loses not only the *Ding an sich* behind a veil of phenomena, but its own self-possession dissolves in temporal incertitude.[24] Derrida says nothing, however, to disprove an eternity that transcends the temporal limitations bounding us. If the "thing" always "escapes," then there must be something that does the escaping. The very notion of being wrong implies something to be wrong about: the apprehension of the wrong assumes the existence of the right. Derrida is only persuasive insofar as we *know* that we do not know.[25]

St. Augustine points out that the inherent fallibility of perception requires that we try to conceive the basis of true perception in a wholly other mode. Even if we could imagine a mind that knew the entire history of the world, past and future alike, as well as one might know a familiar psalm, remembering what was sung, anticipating what remained, such a mind would still be incommensurably inferior to God's. Even a mind with a hypothetically infinite memory and foreknowledge—science fiction's ultimate super computer—would still be bound by time. We must, Augustine urges, think of God's capacity for knowledge in completely different terms:

> You are far, far more marvelous, and far more mysterious. Past and future are not known to you as a well-known psalm to the singer or hearer, whose emotions are changed and sense stretched with the expectation of words to come and the memory of those gone by. Something comes to you as the unalterably eternal; that is, the truly eternal creator of minds. Therefore just as you knew *heaven and earth in the beginning* without any change in your knowledge, even so you made *heaven and earth in the beginning* without any ex-

pansion of your activity. Let him who understands acknowledge you; let him who understands not also acknowledge you.[26]

Derrida successfully shows that logocentric self-identity is a contradiction for a being in the temporal mode, such as man, even for such a being with infinite capacities. But as St. Augustine's discussion indicates, the same strictures do not apply to God who, *by definition*, wholly transcends this spatiotemporal mode. In fact, Derrida's deconstruction of the pretensions of the autonomous, self-identical human subject logically clears the way for an acceptance of the mysterious otherness of the God of Abraham, Isaac, and Jacob. In the face of the demonstrable fragmentation of our being and identity, of the sense of our precarious personhood slipping out of the grasp of differential consciousness, our very existence in any form cries out for some explanation beyond the trace of *différance*—the very slippage itself.

Derrida is certainly someone "who understands," but in this matter his understanding seems impeded by an indisposition to "acknowledge" (or confess or praise). In deploying a rigorous logic with the aim of undermining logic, he makes of himself a comic exemplar of the Cretan liar paradox: A Cretan says, "All Cretans are liars." From the beginning of his deconstructive project, Derrida has been aware of this quandary: "*There is no sense* in doing without the concepts of metaphysics in order to attack metaphysics," he writes in an early essay. "We have no language—no syntax and no lexicon—which is alien to this history; we cannot utter a single destructive proposition which has not already slipped into the form, the logic, and the implicit postulations of precisely what it seeks to contest."[27] As E. Michael Jones observes, Derridean deconstruction, in attacking the hypostatized "intentionalist self" of the Western tradition, merely succeeds in turning language itself into a covert absolute.[28] This conclusion follows inevitably from the notion that *différance*—the metaphysical offspring of the differential structure of the linguistic sign—"includes ontotheology, inscribing it and exceeding it without return."[29]

Robert Magliola maintains that "Derrida's argumentation is *primarily* a critique of *the way we think about* reality and not a judgment of reality"; hence he concludes that Derrida is not an "absurdist."[30] But this seems an overly indulgent view. There is something factitious in Derrida's exposé of the metaphoricity of Western philosophy in the essay, "White Mythology": "Metaphor is less in the philosophical text...than the philosophical text is within metaphor."[31] For the ultimate ontological quest, philosophy's highest truth, as Derrida ceaselessly insists, is theological (or "ontotheological"); and theology's center has always been approachable only in terms of the mode of predication that lies behind metaphor—namely, analogy. Even as God's essence or nature is identical with His act of existing, St. Thomas Aquinas argues, even so His knowledge is identical with His act of knowing. Hence man can no more share God's knowledge and reason than he can share God's existence. It is thus that mankind differs from God. No individual man can exhaust human nature; otherwise there would be no individual men, since individual beings (except for the Divine Being) are less than their natures: "for if in Peter, man and the act of being a man were not different, it would be impossible to predicate 'man' univocally of Peter and Paul, whose acts of existence are different." Evidently the *différance* that Derrida finds infecting human discourse and existence would come as no shock to St. Thomas. Yet this does not mean, St. Thomas continues, that knowledge of God (Derrida's "transcendental signified") is utterly impossible; that all assertions about Him, based on human metaphorical language, are simply capricious: whatever is "predicated of God and creature" is not merely arbitrary or equivocal. "If there were no real likeness of creature to God, then God's essence would not be the image of the creatures, and He would not know them in knowing Himself." This is as much as to say that God would not be God, and the creatures would not be His creatures. Likewise, we could gain no inkling of God, could find no "traces" of Him, in nature; and there could be no distinctions among the arbitrary, equivocal terms that man might apply to God. Therefore, St. Thomas concludes, "…it must be said, that the application of the term 'knowledge' to God's knowledge and to ours is neither altogether univocal nor purely equivocal, but according to analogy, which means nothing else but a proportion."[32]

In this passage from *De Veritate*, St. Thomas considers the two principal targets of Derridean deconstruction: the autonomous, self-identical human subject and the absolute, "logocentric" knowledge of being. St. Thomas specifies the *différance* in human identity; that is, our incompleteness insofar as our existential realization falls short of our essential nature. There is a sense in which what abortionists say about unborn children is true of everyone: we are all only "potentially human." This phrase seems only a compressed formulation of St. Augustine's insight that personal identity is unstable when not supported by grace, an insight most memorably realized in his account of Alypius, who found himself unwillingly enthralled by the spectacle of bloodshed at a gladiatorial show in Carthage: "He was not now the man who had arrived," Augustine writes, "but simply one of the mob to which he had come, and a true companion of those who had brought him."[33] This same distinction has been made by an eminent modern theologian, Hans Urs von Balthasar: "Between that which I actually am or could be or would like or ought to be, and that which I factually live, do, think, judge or experience just now, there gapes an abyss which I can only bridge by virtue of this advance of hope. I never exist completely in my actions and circumstances."[34] In proclaiming the abyss within man's personal self-identity, Derrida seems merely to have rediscovered sin. Moreover, although he may regard Christianity as the ultimate "logocentric ontotheology," it is not the human logos that is placed at the center. "A Christian never has his unity within himself," von Balthasar continues, "nor does he in any way seek it in himself. He does not collect himself around his own center, but rather wholly elsewhere."[35]

Here again is another point at which the current rationalistic, or secular-humanist, critique of postmodernism goes astray. David Lehman quotes with approval the novelist William Gass, who writes in rebuke of Roland Barthes, "The idea of the death of the author does not match the idea of the death of god as perfectly as the current members of the faith suppose, because we know—as they know—that there *are* authors; and we know—as they know—there *are no* gods." Lehman's own comment on this assertion gives the game away: "The 'death of god' is the denial of a metaphysical belief; the 'death of the author' is a denial of a material, historical, verifiable fact."[36] When deconstructionists maintain that the Western intellectual tradition is captive to naïve empiricism, thinkers like Lehman and Gass are a real convenience. They assume that what is "material" and "historical"—a "fact"—is always "verifiable" in a straightforward, uncomplicated way. One can only trust the sensory apprehension and rational ordering of facts, however, if one can trust that the universe itself is reliably orderly, that it makes sense, that it was created by a purposive mind. It is no coincidence, as Stanley Jaki has repeatedly insisted, that modern science originated and developed in the part of the world once called Christendom.[37] There is a touching innocence in the Epicurean faith that the Enlightenment tradition invests in Science—as if it were a wholly autonomous, transcendent activity, not tied to the limits of human reason, presiding benignly over a vast array of facts that fall happily into order by blind chance. Even to think clearly about the matter for a moment demonstrates that neither the mind of man nor the physical universe in which he lives are self-sustaining or self-explanatory. On this point deconstruction is right: let God truly "die" and the author—along with his *authority*—must also die.

Given the dependence of human rationality on the Divine Reason, of which it is the image and likeness, it is no scandal, at least not for the Christian, that metaphysical discourse is imperfect and oblique—that, in Derrida's words, "the philosophical text is within metaphor." To know Being—absolute, necessary Being, as distinct from its contingent, created reflections—is to know God. As St. Thomas points out, God's very nature implies that it be impossible for man to make univocal predications regarding his Maker, to capture either the divine essence or existence in human words. Language is the medium of human knowledge, and both language and knowledge are necessarily curbed by the intrinsic limitations of human existence. But just because *différance*, the "undecidable trace," haunts our discourse, it cannot therefore be inferred that the same *différance* infiltrates everything about which we think and speak. Our central metaphysical knowledge is neither univocal nor equivocal, but analogical: it is incomplete, indirect, in a sense metaphorical. It is not simply meaningless or mistaken. The very terms "meaningless" and "mistaken" require the concepts of meaning and accuracy in order to signify. Further, the signifier cannot operate without the signified, even if the latter can be regarded as absent and inaccessible. As C. S. Lewis quips, "the *Romance of the Rose* could not, without loss, be rewritten as the *Romance of the Onion*."[38] Neither the rose nor the onion *is* (or is the same as) the erotic favor of a beautiful lady, but the former provides the better analogy. If Derrida were altogether right, if language were altogether equivocal, if the signifier/signified relationship of the sign were altogether collapsed, then there would be no way of distinguishing between romantic roses and onions. Where Derrida is right, of course, is in seeing that the rose is not finally the lady, and the lady sometimes turns into the tiger. Or we may say, theology is not faith, much less the beatific vision; and this amounts to saying that Derrida's principal discovery is that man is not God. In the wake of the Enlightenment and mankind's conquest of nature by means of empirical science and technology, Derrida's discovery is not trivial.

As Robert Magliola points out, according to Derrida, "Any philosophy of presence can be disproven. The contradictory which unseats the conclusion of a philosophy of presence is also illogical."[39] The law of noncontradiction can perhaps be contradicted in the sense that reason can stumble against its own limits and recognize that its final certainties are matters of intuition, not evidence. Only faith can sustain the mind above the abyss that opens up before naked human reason, and faith can only be a gift, the work of grace.

How curious it is, then, that Derrida and the deconstructionists are generally reticent about the channels of grace, the sacraments; for the sacraments, especially the Eucharist, are the ultimate affirmation in the face of deconstruction's "pure negative reference." Deconstruction is a philosophy that insists that all discourse is always the sign of an absence, that the signifier marks the absent presence of the signified. From the earliest times, Christianity has found the ultimate Real Presence—what Derrida calls the "Transcendental Signified"—in Holy Communion.[40] In the sacraments of the New Covenant, grace is not merely *signified* or *prefigured*, as in the ceremonies of the Old Covenant; in the New Covenant grace is contained and conferred: word, material sign (for instance, bread and wine), and grace all converge in the Presence of the Word. And the sacraments are made possible by the Incarnation, Passion, Death, and

Resurrection of the Word, the divine Logos.[41] The Eucharist is especially significant in this regard in that the Church teaches that Jesus Christ, true God and true man, is "really and substantially contained under the appearance of the sensible signs."[42] The doctrine of the Real Presence in this sacrament is thus the fulfillment of the Messianic promise of the Old Covenant, the promise of Emmanuel, "God with us."

One might argue that Derrida is thus true to his Jewish heritage, which is *par excellence* the religion of scripture—of writing—and of the deferral of the Presence of the Word—the *Parousia*.[43] He might also be regarded as the last scion of the Protestant Reformation with its tendency to displace the sacraments by an intense emphasis on the written word—*sola scriptura*. Derrida, however, would seem to have taken these developments beyond the limits of Judaism or Protestantism: he is a Moses who has broken the Tablets and will not reascend the mountain, who offers only more wandering—more *erring*—in the wilderness, with the Promised Land endlessly deferred.[44]

Derrida's writing at least has the merit of unveiling the actual results of the secularization of Western philosophy and culture during the past several centuries. In exposing the covert dependency of all "logocentric" metaphysics on the concept of God, even when God's personal reality has been rejected, Derrida demonstrates the emptiness, indeed the fraudulence of profane humanism. He proffers a choice between the deconstructionist abyss and the fullness of grace, between Derrida or Deity. Regrettably, Derrida's revelation seems to have been unintentional, and he seems to have gathered no wisdom from his own insights. What is lurking in the abyss is what has always been lurking there, although it has different names at different times and in different places. One of its names in the contemporary academic world turned out to be Paul de Man, Derrida's deceased colleague. At a memorial service for de Man at Yale early in 1984, Barbara Johnson summed up the prevailing view among the mourners with these words: "In a profession full of fakeness, he was real."[45] But in fact, de Man was the consummate fake. Not only had he written anti-Semitic articles for a collaborationist newspaper in Nazi-occupied Brussels, he had then bankrupted his father and fled Belgium, leaving behind a host of angry, unpaid creditors. Once in the United States he abandoned his common-law wife and three children in order to marry an American graduate student, thereby securing a place in this country. Ironically, the Jewish Derrida has been foremost in manufacturing excuses for his erstwhile colleague.[46] As David Lehman remarks, "The lesson of the de Man affair has less to do with the unmasking of a scoundrel than with the stubborn refusal of his followers to read the writing on the wall, to read it as it is written, and to understand its import."[47]

It is fitting that the role assumed by Derrida and deconstruction in regard to literary theory be illustrated by a literary character: it then becomes clear that the measure of deconstruction had been taken by the imaginative vision of literature before the theory had "a local habitation and a name." In Flannery O'Connor's "A Good Man Is Hard to Find," an ordinary, middle-class American family, driving through rural Georgia, falls into the clutches of an escaped murderer. While his two companions are methodically shooting the father, the mother, and the two children, the grandmother, a "respectable," and rather shallow, Christian lady, pleads for her life: "Pray! Jesus, you ought not to shoot a lady. I'll give you all the money I've got!"[48] The Misfit is not interested in the offer of money ("Lady, ...there never was a body that give the undertaker a tip"), but he is obsessed with Jesus:

> "Jesus was the only One that ever raised the dead," The Misfit continued, "and He shouldn't have done it. He thrown

everything off balance. If He did what He said, then it's
nothing for you to do but throw away everything and follow
Him, and if He didn't, then it's nothing for you to do but
enjoy the few minutes you got left the best way you can—
by killing somebody or burning down his house or doing
some other meanness to him. No pleasure but meanness,"
he said and his voice had become almost a snarl.

In her terror the grandmother comes near to despair. Confronted
with death, her routine, unreflective faith is put to a severe and
apparently crippling test:

> "Maybe He didn't raise the dead," the old lady mumbled,
> not knowing what she was saying and feeling so dizzy that
> she sank down in the ditch with her legs twisted under her.

It is the murderer, however, who is the victim of genuine despair,
and his miserable perdition is the occasion for the grandmother's
crucial epiphany:

> "I wasn't there so I can't say He didn't," The Misfit said. "I
> wisht I had of been there," he said, hitting the ground with
> his fist. "It ain't right I wasn't there because if I had of been
> there I would of known. Listen lady," he said in a high voice,
> "if I had of been there I would of known and I wouldn't be
> like I am now." His voice seemed about to crack and the
> grandmother's head cleared for an instant. She saw the man's
> face twisted close to her own as if he were going to cry and
> she murmured, "Why you're one of my babies. You're one
> of my own children!" She reached out and touched him on
> the shoulder. The Misfit sprang back as if a snake had bitten
> him and shot her three times through the chest. Then he put
> his gun down on the ground and took off his glasses and

began to clean them.

The grandmother, we are told, "half sat and half lay in a puddle of blood with her legs crossed under her like a child's and her face smiling up at the cloudless sky." The term "child" could be deconstructed in Derridean fashion. The suggestion of spiritual immaturity it conveys could be construed to undermine the sign of new-found innocence acquired in her sudden but telling acknowledgment of her own sinfulness in recognizing her "kinship" with The Misfit. Or this relationship could make her the Devil's mother, and The Misfit, who is often right, may be right in recoiling from her as from a "snake." On the other hand, one could argue that her confession of parentage restores her childhood hopes. These are doubtless just a few of the possible interpretations available in the text, but they do not amount to mere "dissemination."[49] The deconstructive attempt to deny the uniqueness of imaginative literature and to unravel every text into tatters is overwhelmed by the mysterious power of fiction, exemplified in O'Connor's story, to make meanings coalesce rather than fragment and dissipate. The *childish* old woman in a moment of revelation becomes *childlike*. The coherence that holds these contrary terms together is disclosed in the grim alternative to her humiliation and death registered in the exchange between The Misfit and one of his henchmen that closes the story:

> "She was a talker, wasn't she?" Bobby Lee said, sliding down in the ditch with a yodel.
>
> "She would of been a good woman," The Misfit said, "if it had been somebody to shoot her every minute of her life."
>
> "Some fun!" Bobby Lee said.
>
> "Shut up, Bobby Lee," The Misfit said. "It's no real pleasure in life."

Like The Misfit, Derrida wasn't there when Jesus raised the dead, so he has made a career of killing the Logos and burning down the house of reason; and since the disclosure of Paul de Man's wartime activities as pro-Nazi journalist, he must have begun to feel, "It's no real pleasure in life." Christians, however, and indeed anyone who cherishes the power of the Word, stand in need of the world's Derridas to shoot them every minute of their lives. Salvation lies, not in the theological equivalent of being a lady, but rather in faith in Jesus. Moreover, all literature, not just that which we call Scripture, reminds us of the limitations of human reason—a lesson sorely needed since the Enlightenment. Perhaps one can no more argue with Derrida than with The Misfit; there is certainly no arguing with death. Still, even as poetry requires what Alexander Pope calls "a grace beyond the reach of art," so human life yearns for an illumination of grace, a stirring of charity, which seems to be what the grandmother experiences at her life's close. Finally, heirs of the Western tradition must remember that Derrida, like The Misfit, is one of our own children. He is the manifestation of what happens when philosophic reason is drained of religious faith, and he is right about the alienated, deconstructed, angst-ridden postmodern world: "It's no real pleasure in life"—unless you "throw away everything and follow Him."

CHAPTER THREE

Deconstruction and the Fear and Loathing of Logos

Despite his preëminent role in establishing deconstruction in the foreground of modern literary theory and in thus rearranging the landscape of contemporary academic life, Jacques Derrida is really less a genuine innovator than a superb publicist. His ideas are hardly without precedent, and rivals as well as collaborators have advanced into the same forbidding territory by different routes. "A quantum of strength," writes Friedrich Nietzsche, "is equivalent to a quantum of urge, will, activity, and it is only the snare of language (of the arch-fallacies of reason petrified in language), presenting all activity as conditioned by an agent—the 'subject'— that blinds us to this fact.... But no such agent exists; there is no 'being' behind the doing, acting, becoming; the 'doer' has simply been added to the deed by the imagination—the doing is every-thing."[1] In this remark and scores of others like it, recurring throughout his works like hiccoughs, the "project" of deconstructing Western metaphysics has already attained a fairly unambiguous articulation. Being is alienated from act; reason is alienated from language. The Word, or Logos, through whom all things were made, according to the Fourth Gospel and the Nicene Creed, is alienated from the Creation; that is, the world ceases to be patterned after wisdom, and reality loses its nature. This dismantling of our metaphysical grip on reality is not without practical consequences, as Nietzsche subsequently points out by invoking the slogan of "the invincible Society of Assassins": "'Nothing is true; everything is permitted.' Here we have real freedom, for the notion of truth itself has been disposed of."[2]

Nietzsche is worth pausing over. He is probably the most important—surely he is the most vociferous—philosophic ancestor of contemporary deconstruction; and in such passages this slippery term, while it is not defined, is at least revealed; and the implications of its "project" spelled out quite plainly. Any notion of rational authority or wisdom is simply discounted; reason is understood to be the servant of desire's restless energy. Deconstruction is, then, the effort of reason to devour itself and hence the limits or constraints that rationality necessarily discovers in the finite human condition. For this reason, deconstruction is a crucial factor in postmodern theory in all its varied guises. Despite the rancorous altercations among Marxists, feminists, new historicists, neo-Freudians, and every position across the ideological spectrum, all are united in a virulent antihumanism that despises the concept of human nature precisely as the image and likeness of God; that is, as man's rationality is the sign of his participation in the divine order—in the Logos. In its relentless attack upon the "ontotheology" and "logocentricism" of the Western tradition, deconstruction currently provides the common factor among the divergent manifestations of secularized man's recoil from the Logos as the pattern of normative rationality.

Liddell and Scott's *Greek-English Lexicon* fills up the better part of three large double-column pages with fine print to define the word λόγος—surely one of the key terms of Western civilization. It marks the convergence of Hellenic conceptions of ground, reason, and discourse with the Hebraic personification of the Word and Wisdom of God, in the New Testament identified with the Second Person of the Trinity, incarnate in Christ Jesus. Regarded as the formal principle of the cosmos in one perspective and the means of its creation and conservation in the other, it guarantees that in Western civilization reality will be endowed with an intelligible, purposive structure; that is, both the material nature of the world and its historical development will be meaningful. In conjunction with the Greek tragic sense and the Judaeo-Christian concept of Original Sin, this conception of the order and purpose of the universe provides an explanation both of meaning and absurdity, of joy and sorrow, of triumph and tragedy. In other words, it furnishes the basis of all normative criteria, which culminate in our understanding of good and evil.

As the author of *Beyond Good and Evil* (a rubric appropriate for virtually all his writings), Nietzsche is necessarily the enemy of all norms and standards—not, mind you, of this or that law or rule, but of the idea of the normative, even of the normal. A further consequence is that Nietzsche must be the enemy of meaning, for to have meaning is to have significance; that is, to *bear a sign*, to be *marked*, to be this thing and not another, to be distinguished from and placed in relation to other things. The meaning of an entity is thus the basis of its identity, which entails definition, discrimination, judgment. It is intellectual law and order. To know these distinctions and to know the reason that unites them in an overall pattern is to know reality, and the actual nature of reality is, then, the truth. The central religious tradition of the West teaches that knowledge of the truth is freedom (John 8.32), but Nietzsche teaches, to the contrary, that truth is an obstacle to "real freedom." For if truth exists—if things have meaning and purpose; if they have ontological integrity—then everything is *not* permitted.

Nietzsche's crucial importance in the unhinging of metaphysics is that he went about it so explicitly. It is plausible to assign responsibility for the disruption of the classical and Christian tradition to various philosophic developments, from the nominalism of William of Ockham to the subjectivization of metaphysics by Immanuel Kant; but it was Nietzsche who openly declared war on the Western understanding of reason. The contribution of Jacques Derrida was to make Nietzsche's call for intellectual anarchy into a viable academic research project. Derrida exhibits a certain shrewdness in stigmatizing the philosophy and learning of the Western world as "logocentric." Rhetorically, the term is effective insofar as it creates discomfort in the secularized heirs of Enlightenment rationalism by reminding them of the indisputable connection between human reason, or logos, and the divine Logos. To admit to "logocentricism" is adroitly made to seem the equivalent in academic circles of being identified as a biblical literalist or "creationist."[3] The term also fairly specifies Derrida's target, for it is precisely the center that he would deny. Or to change metaphors, language's foundation in the Logos is undermined, its mooring severed. Language as the utterance of a self-present subject is displaced into the pure supplementarity of writing or textuality:

> The surrogate does not substitute itself for anything which has somehow preexisted it. From then on it was probably necessary to begin to think that there was no center, that the center could not be thought of in the form of a being-present, that the center had no natural locus, that it was not a fixed locus, but a function, a sort of non-locus in which an infinite number of sign-substitutions came into play. This moment was that in which language invaded the universal problem-

atic; that in which, in the absence of center or origin, everything became discourse—provided we can agree on this
word—that is to say, when everything became a system where
the central signified, the original or transcendental signified, is never absolutely present outside a system of differences. The absence of the transcendental signified extends
the domain and the interplay of signification *ad infinitum.*[4]

The normative matrix radiating out from the central Logos is
superseded by what Derrida calls "free play"—a game without
rules, with reality up for grabs. But although the foundation has
been sapped, the edifice is, in some sense, left standing. Rather
than a frontal assault on metaphysics, Derrida proposes subversion
from within. Acknowledging his kinship to such revolutionary
ancestors as Nietzsche, Freud, and Heidegger, Derrida nevertheless concedes that they were all "trapped in a sort of circle," albeit
a circle without a center. Evidently, the literally *illogical* chaos of
deconstruction cannot be negotiated without setting up temporary
landmarks built out of the debris of traditional philosophy:

> *There is no sense* in doing without the concepts of metaphys-
> ics in order to attack metaphysics. We have no language—
> no syntax and no lexicon—which is alien to this history; we
> cannot utter a single destructive proposition which has not
> already slipped into the form, the logic, and the implicit
> postulations of precisely what it seeks to contest.[5]

There is indeed no sense in doing without concepts; however,
the postmodern muse is an enchantress, and the spell of her melody
is pervasive in current literary study. Deconstruction provides the
underlying theme of this siren song, and while it can be heard in the
work of an acknowledged deconstructionist like Paul de Man, it is

escapable in the idiosyncratic theories of Harold Bloom and the neo-Freudian psychoanalysis of Jacques Lacan, who has exercised an incalculable influence on feminist literary theory. Decon-struction is in many ways a symptom of the cultural pathology of our time, but it is also a powerful analytic tool, which has captivated a good many keen minds. The term *heresy* comes from a Greek word αἵρεσις meaning "choice"; the heretic might be said to be someone who is *choosy* about his religion. He typically exalts a few "choice" truths, or aspects of truth, while discarding what he does not fancy. Deconstruction is like all successful heresies in laying hold of a compelling truth and exploiting it in a critical situation. After several centuries during which the moral and spiritual traditions of Western civilization have eroded in the face of relentless secularization—a secularization that is often little more than a dilution and sentimen-talization of the Judaeo-Christian tradition—the human condition is beginning once more to seem intrinsically grim. Having gnawed away the structural supports of Western civilization, the rodents of secular humanism now have nothing to offer us but a pile of sawdust. In these circumstances, the message that proclaims the city of man a ruin on the verge of collapse can be exhilarating as well as powerful.

One such message is delivered by Paul de Man. As noted in the preceding chapter, de Man was involved in rather dubious activities as a young man during World War II; however, such lasting damage as he may have done to Western civilization has been effected more by means of his academic work in America, which brought him fame and success rather than opprobrium, than by what he did in occu-pied Belgium. Although he sought to conceal and distance himself from his Nazi associations of the past, de Man was very openly and proudly part of what might be called the ideological "occupation" of the contemporary university. Deconstruction may be regarded as the distilled intellectual essence of the totalitarian ideologies of the

modern world—the full disclosure of their nihilistic essence be-
neath the veneer of factitious economics or racial politics: there is no
God, no real distinction between good and evil, no meaning or
purpose to human life. It is the world "demystified" by the Condi-
tioners described by C. S. Lewis: "The impulse to scratch when I itch
or to pull to pieces when I am inquisitive is immune from the solvent
which is fatal to my justice, or honour, or care for posterity. When
all that says 'it is good' has been debunked, what says 'I want' remains."[6] That which does remain, then, is the violent exercise of raw
power or the languorous feast of despair, but this attitude of unblink-
ing disillusionment is not without a fey attraction.

The appeal can be gauged by placing a liberal Victorian account
of the poet Percy Shelley beside de Man's. Edward Dowden warns
us against being taken in by the "charm" of Matthew's Arnold's famous
description of Shelley as "A beautiful and ineffectual angel, beating
in the void his luminous wings in vain," and then proceeds to shape
a rococo figurine of Shelley, which would sit very nicely among the
other china knick-knacks on the parlor mantelpiece:

> He was too young to have learned the lessons of experience
> derived from the facts of the French Revolution, as they
> developed themselves from day to day. He accepted the
> doctrine of *Aufklärung* from Godwin's "Political Justice" with
> awed and delighted mind. With Condorcet he beheld as in
> a vision the endless progress of the human race. His dreams
> were bright and generous dreams of youth, and in truth they
> were not altogether of a baseless fabric. Much that has be-
> come actual in the nineteenth century has grown out of the
> visions and aspirations of the age of revolution; much per-
> haps remains to be realized.[7]

Thus Shelley the lyrical singer can be happily enjoyed in middle-class domestic comfort, while the more alarming implications of his beliefs and actions are tactfully glossed over. This attitude to a truly menacing figure recalls the *bonhomie* that we were all exhorted by the mass media to invest in the celebrations of the bicentennial of the French Revolution—or as one television commentator put it, the bicentennial *of France*—as if France had not existed until two hundred years ago, when it was born in the throes of ideological genocide, that characteristically modern phenomenon. By the same token, Dowden assures us that Shelley was "religious" in the characteristically modern sense of the word: "His atheism was the denial of a creator rather than the denial of a living spirit of the universe. A Christian he never became in the theological sense of that word; but certainly, at a later time, he deeply reverenced the personal character of Jesus."[8]

Dowden furnishes an instance—quite extreme, to be sure—of the approach to Shelley and Romanticism that de Man deprecates in a late essay on *The Triumph of Life*, a poem left in fragmentary condition by Shelley's early death by drowning. "For what we have done to the dead Shelley," de Man complains, "and with all the other dead bodies that appear in romantic literature...is simply to bury them, to bury them in their own texts made into epitaphs and monumental graves." That is, criticism and scholarship have conferred upon Shelley's unfinished text and upon all the chaotic fragments of "romantic literature" a spurious completeness and unity: "They have been transformed into historical and aesthetic objects." Not that de Man expects or even wishes that scholarly and critical activity should cease: "No degree of knowledge can ever stop this madness, for it is the madness of words." The problem comes in the effort to take critical insights or scholarly conclusions seriously: "What *would* be naïve is to believe that this strategy, which is not *our* strategy, since we are its product rather than its agent, can be a source of value and has to be celebrated or denounced accordingly."[9]

De Man develops a view of Shelley that responds with great sensitivity to the dark underside of Romanticism, to its anxious and outraged realization—despite its vision of "the endless progress of the human race," despite its "bright and generous dreams of youth"— that man is still mortal. "In Shelley's absence," de Man writes, "the task of thus reinscribing the disfiguration now devolves entirely on the reader. The final test of reading, in *The Triumph of Life*, depends on how one reads the textuality of this event [the poet's death], how one disposes of Shelley's body." It turns out that once we have disposed of God as creator, "the living spirit of the universe" is not sufficient to endow that universe with meaning in the face of death:

> Attempts to define, to understand or to circumscribe romanticism in relation to ourselves and in relation to other literary movements are all part of this naïve belief [in criticism and value judgment]. *The Triumph of Life* warns us that nothing, whether deed, word, thought or text, ever happens in relation, positive or negative, to anything that precedes, follows or exists elsewhere, but only as a random event whose power, like the power of death, is due to the randomness of its occurrence.[10]

This is no mean interpretation of Shelley, for all that it stresses the absence of meaning. Dowden's vague pieties about the "living spirit of the universe" are no substitute for the Logos, and de Man is much closer to the real implications of Shelley's atheism.

In the process of unveiling Shelley, he also discloses the motives of deconstruction as well as the source of its fascination for many contemporary thinkers. The power of deconstruction and the literary ideologies associated with it is the power of the abyss. It is the power of sheer disillusion and negation: "Practical criticism, in France and in the United States, functions more and more as a demystification of the belief that literature is a privileged language."[11] All that distinguishes literature in de Man's view is a negative feature: "It is the only form of language free from the fallacy of unmediated expression." Hence literature only exists as a signifier for the failure of signification: "The self-reflecting mirror-effect by means of which a work of fiction asserts, by its very existence, its separation from empirical reality, its divergence, as a sign, from meaning that depends for its existence on the constitutive activity of this sign characterizes the work of literature in its essence." De Man quotes the character Julie, in Rousseau's *La Nouvelle Heloïse*, on the superior suitability of "the country of chimeras" for human habitation and in praise of the beauty of "what is not." It turns out that Rousseau provides even more provocative occasions for deconstruction than Shelley. De Man acknowledges with weary tolerance the inclination of ordinary folk to regard Rousseau as "deluded," then dismisses the notion:

> But one hesitates to use terms such as nostalgia or desire to designate this kind of consciousness, for all nostalgia or desire is desire of something or for someone; here, the consciousness does not result from the absence of something, but consists of the presence of nothingness. Poetic language names this void with ever-renewed understanding and, like Rousseau's longing, it never tires of naming it again. This persistent naming is what we call literature.[12]

Paul de Man on the subject of literature sounds very much like Flannery O'Connor's one-legged philosopher, Hulga/Joy Hopewell, on the subject of love: "But it's not a word I use. I don't have illusions. I'm one of those people who see *through* to nothing."[13] Fortunately for de Man, his comparative literature classes at Yale were unlikely to throw him into contact with many itinerant Bible salesmen. Hence he was free to proffer a supersubtle, almost sublimated version of the nineteenth-century effort to make a religion out of poetry, which would displace Christianity. In Rousseau he finds a model for turning absence and nothingness into ironic idols—ironic because he recognizes that the worship of a substitute God is futile. "You made us for yourself," writes St. Augustine, "and our heart is restless until it rest in you."[14] Similarly, St. Thomas argues at length that man's ultimate and only unmixed happiness consists in the eternal contemplation of God.[15] De Man seems to agree with Augustine and Thomas in finding this life deficient, and his idea that literature is an expression of man's longing in the face of this emptiness is certainly not incompatible with the traditional Christian view. De Man, however, will not shake off the spell of the abyss, the decadent indulgence in the melancholy of despair. He represents deconstruction in its purest form as the disillusionment and despondency of secular humanism: he ruthlessly smashes the Enlightenment idols that man has carved out of his own mind and is left breathing clouds of marble dust in the ruined temple.

If there is something rather wan, even fey, in the lucubrations of Paul de Man, Harold Bloom takes essentially the same data and constructs the most aggressive and robustly self-aggrandizing critical practice of our time. If knowledge fails, there is always sheer will—the drive to psychic power and satisfaction. Bloom is an avowed modern Gnostic who regards *gnosis* more as a matter of freedom to dominate than as knowledge in the traditional sense: "Freedom, in a poem, must mean freedom of meaning, the freedom to have a meaning of one's own. Such freedom is wholly illusory unless it is achieved against a prior plenitude of meaning, which is tradition, and so also against language." The work of literature is not, then, a representation or vision of reality; it is a site, a psychological locus,

where the ego seeks to realize—to make reality of—its own fantasies: "Reading well is a struggle because fictions and poems can only
be defined, at their best, as works that are bound to be misread, that
is to say, troped by the reader."[16]

But if the "strong" reader inevitably does violence to the text,
he has merely imitated the violence of the "strong" but "belated"
poet struggling against the oppressiveness of the literary tradition.
The almost universal tendency to regard aesthetic activity as set apart
from ordinary practical concerns ("Even Freud, like all the rest of us,
idealized the arts....") is merely a naïve illusion:

> Because of such prevalent idealization, we all of us still resist
> the supposed stigma of identifying the poet's drive towards
> immortality with the triadic sequence of narcissism, wounded
> self-regard, and aggression. But change in poetry and criti-
> cism as in any human endeavor comes about only through
> aggression.[17]

The entirety of literary activity is thus reduced to the sublimation
of the darker psychic drives: "Poetry, like criticism, is conflict and
crisis, is projected jealousy and the death drive, is the horror and
allure of incest."[18] The final source of poetry, however, is the same
as it is in de Man; poetry—all literature—is the alternative to a
terrified howl of anguish in the face of mortality, of the utter
emptiness of the abyss:

> Freedom and lying are intimately associated in belated
> poetry, and the notion that contains them both might best
> be named "evasion." Evasion is a process of avoiding, a way
> of escaping, but also it is an excuse. Usage has tinged the
> word with a certain stigma, but in our poetry what is being
> evaded ultimately is fate, particularly the necessity of dying.[19]

As in the work of Nietzsche and de Man, so in Bloom the Truth does not set you free; freedom is the ability to deny or "evade" the Truth. Hence literature is not a representation of reality; it is an escape from reality.

Bloom prefers to distance himself from deconstruction and says, with a sniff of disdain, "I reject all Gallic modes of recent interpretation because they dehumanize poetry and criticism"; and, though he also declines to "espouse a sentimental humanism," he nonetheless admits to enjoying the allegation: "I find it lunatic but cheerful that the deconstructionists call me a sentimental humanist, while traditional academics, like my distinguished mentor M. H. Abrams, refer to me as insisting upon theories that are human—all-too-human."[20] Bloom undertakes to rehabilitate presence as "what Emerson and Shelley called *power*, and to call the power of strong poetry or strong criticism an illusion is to raise again the eternal issue of the relation of poetry to human action." The implication of these words seems to be that the charge of illusion can be discounted because true knowledge does not matter anyway—because the faculty of knowing always serves the urgency of the will. "Poetry and criticism alike usurp strength," Bloom continues, "only by invoking the language of desire, possession, and power, and such language, to me, seems inevitably the language of Gnosis."[21]

Bloom purports to construct by means of Gnostic theorizing a more tough-minded and "realistic" account of the human situation than is to be had in orthodox Judaism or Christianity or in traditional Western moral philosophy. The Freudian view of the unconscious is substituted for the concept of Original Sin, and instead of human nature being understood as fallen, to be fallen is held to be our nature; to be abnormal the norm:

Thus human sexuality, alas, on this account has not had, from its very origins, any real object. The only real object was milk, which belongs to the vital order. Hence the sorrows and authentic anguish of all human erotic quest, hopelessly seeking to rediscover an object, which never was the true object anyway. All human sexuality is thus tropological, whereas we all of us desperately need and long for it to be literal.

What Bloom is calling "human sexuality" turns out to be no more real than literature: "our sexuality is a continual crisis, which I would now say is not so much mimicked or parodied by the High Romantic crisis poem, but rather our sexuality itself is a mimickry or parody of statelier action of the will which is figured forth in the characteristic Post-Enlightenment strong poem."[22] Although Bloom attempts to distinguish his criticism from deconstruction and other "Gallic modes of recent interpretation" by a reaffirmation of the ties between poetry and "human action," he only succeeds in diminishing the distinction between literature and life—a typically deconstructive move—and reducing the reality of something so thoroughly human as erotic desire. Bloom posits an equivocal relationship between poetry and sexuality: both lack a real object.

But he has told us already that poetry and criticism are together a means of evading fate, and, in another passage, "The idealization of power in the reading process, or processes, is finally a last brutal idealization, a noble lie against our own origins. This lie is against mortality...."[23] But the evasion of death necessarily entails the evasion of life insofar as it is anchored in a reality apart from human wishing. The consequences of Bloom's willful evasiveness are nowhere more apparent than in his reading of Wallace Stevens' "The Course of a Particular." This brief lyric is a characteristic manifestation of the poet's bleak vision of a natural universe utterly alien to human concerns and sentiments. The poem opens with an equivocation fraught with irony:

Today the leaves cry, hanging on branches swept by wind,
Yet the nothingness of winter becomes a little less.
It is still full of icy shades and shapen snow.[24]

Does the "nothingness" become "a little less" because it becomes more of or more like something? Or does even nothingness itself lessen, become still less than what it already was? The next two tercets somewhat reluctantly explore the possibilities of finding in the "cry" of the leaves—a cry confined to "today"—some minimal hint of meaning. Perhaps the sound of the leaves embodies a sense, a message "concerning someone else." But it seems a fruitless undertaking despite a conventional wish to find harmonious correspondence in the universe—"though one says that one is part of everything." The final two tercets of the lyric assert definitively that the "cry" has meaning only in human fantasy:

The leaves cry. It is not a cry of divine attention,
Nor the smoke-drift of puffed-out heroes, nor human cry.
It is the cry of leaves that do not transcend themselves,

In the absence of fantasia, without meaning more
Than they are in the final finding of the ear, in the thing
Itself, until, at last, the cry concerns no one at all.

Plainly this is a poem of disillusionment, by one of the last poets of the Romantic tradition, with the Romantic visionary's espousal of nature's self-transcendence, or, in M. H. Abrams' phrase, "natural supernaturalism."[25] Harold Bloom is, of course, too shrewd a critic not to see this, but he refuses to accept it. "The fiction of the leaves," he writes, "has become the only available image of voice, the last remnant of the human in a landscape of loss, of the possibility of mere force without meaning. Stevens makes the gesture of seeming to accept such force, but his poem belies him throughout."[26] Now it is certainly true that a poem can mean more, or even something other, than what the poet consciously intended at the time of the composition; but Bloom is not taking issue with a comment by the poet external to and later than the poem, but the primary thrust of the poem's own text. Such an undertaking requires great sensitivity to shadings of language and scrupulous attention to detail; however, Bloom willfully misjudges the tone. He points out (correctly) that the line, "And though one says that one is part of everything," is an allusion to Whitman, but he simply ignores the ironic, dismissive quality of the phrasing, especially in the arch use of the stilted pronoun, "one." Whitman's expansive secular faith in an autonomous self's sufficiency to invest physical nature with animation and meaning is evoked only to be rejected. Likewise, Bloom fails to acknowledge that the triple repetition of the phrase, "the leaves cry," becomes only a dead mechanism by reiteration, not an intimation of voice.

In the end Bloom has to wrench Stevens' poem away from its faithfulness to the truth of experience, its commitment to "the thing / Itself": "Leaves that do not transcend themselves do not cry out. If fantasia is really absent, then Stevens is hallucinating, but fantasia is indeed present, as Stevens wills in spite of his own will." The factitious distinction between fantasia and hallucination—the latter is never an issue in the poem—merely serves to disguise the inescapable fact that the "cry"—understood as an utterance—is in the consciousness of the perceiver, not in the leaves. Bloom takes a poem that confronts the reality of a universe perceived as godless and tries to turn it into an "evasion": "The words of his poem belie his poem's lie against time, but the lie against time...is stronger." In his closing sentences Bloom virtually concedes that his "reading" of "The Course of a Particular" is an act of appropriation, an effort to recruit the poem for the Gnostic apotheosis of the self that would impose its will upon the nature of things: "The cry may concern no one at all, except the strong reader, who will turn the leaves of Stevens' book and in that turning transume another cry, and yet another, in that work we are not required to complete, yet neither are we free to abandon."[27] The task cannot be completed because it is innately impossible: the reality of death is ineluctable. It cannot be abandoned because that would be to acknowledge either that nature is devoid of human significance, or that it is the Creator, not the creature, who endows the creation with meaning and purpose. Stevens himself finally recognized the limitations of human will and desire. Before his death the poet was received into the Catholic Church, an event the critic neglects to mention.[28] Although Harold Bloom wishes to separate himself from the deconstructionists, he shares their aversion to "logocentricism" and recoils from the Logos for the same motive, that men are subject to a divinely ordained reality and not the fabricators of their own transcendent realm.

Unlike Harold Bloom, Jacques Lacan has never been accused of "sentimental humanism," although he is another principal source of Freudian influence on current literary theory. It is surely a curious state of affairs when many American English departments have been so powerfully affected by a French psychoanalyst. There is also a certain irony in the fact that the appeal of Lacan's thought has been most forceful among feminist theoreticians. Given the central role of masculine Oedipal conflicts in Freud's psychoanalytic theory, as well as his treatment of feminine sexuality in terms of "penis envy," it would hardly seem likely that a Neo-Freudian would escape the feminist censure visited upon his mentor. Oddly enough, it is precisely Lacan's emphasis on the phallus as "the privileged signifier" that both accommodates his thought to radical feminism and provides the weaponry for his assault on the very concept of human nature.

First it must be noted that in Lacan's version of Freud "phallus" does not mean "penis"; indeed, the relation between the two terms is at most tangential, almost accidental:

> In Freudian doctrine, the phallus is not a fantasy, if what is understood by that is an imaginary effect. Nor is it as such an object (part, internal, good, bad, etc....) insofar as this term tends to accentuate the reality involved in a relationship. It is even less the organ, penis or clitoris, which it symbolizes. And it is not incidental that Freud took his reference for it from the simulacrum which it represented for the Ancients.[29]

In classical antiquity the *phallus* was a large, monstrous image of the *membrum virile*; a symbol of the generative power of nature, it was borne along in processions during Dionysiac orgies. According to St. Augustine, "it was necessary for the most honorable matron of a household to place a crown publicly on this dishonorable member."[30] Some contemporary feminists seem to wish to play the part of the matron. According to Lacan and his feminist adherents, in Freudian psychoanalysis the phallus represents an undifferentiated desire—an irrational want or demand for which there is no specific object, and for which no biological or natural satisfaction is possible. The phallus is thus virtually a transcendent term in an interpretation of the human condition that denies transcendence.

Lacan's crucial step is to reinterpret Freud in terms of Saussurian linguistics; this move results in "what is perhaps his most startling conclusion, that *the structure of the unconscious is the structure of language.*"[31]

In this schema, "The phallus is the privileged signifier of that mark where the share of logos is wedded to the advent of desire." It "can only play its role as veiled, that is, as in itself the sign of the latency with which everything signifiable is struck as soon as it is raised (*aufgehoben*) to the function of signifier." As a signifier the phallus has nothing to do with what is substantially or definably masculine; it is only an arbitrary mark of difference. As re-presentation it defers presence and is thus a mark of absence: "The phallus is the signifier of this *Aufhebung* itself which it inaugurates (initiates) by its own disappearance."[32]

This may all seem a trifle *recherché*, but as one commentator cheerily puts it, "the advantage of Lacan's approach is that it gets away from biological determinism and puts Freudian psychoanalysis in touch with the social system (through language)."[33] Now there is more at stake in this airy dismissal of "biological determinism" than a reproof to B. F. Skinner: it is the apotheosis of the popular feminist slogan, "Biology is not destiny." According to Juliet Mitchell, "The structure and content of the *Three Essays* [Freud's *Three Essays on the Theory of Sexuality*] erodes any idea of normative sexuality. By deduction, if no heterosexual attraction is ordained in nature, there can be no genderised sex—there cannot at the outset be a male or female person in a psychological sense." Appeals to anatomy and physiology are dismissed out of hand: "There is never a causal relationship between the biological urge and its representative: we cannot perceive an activity and deduce behind it a corresponding physical motive force."[34] In other words, since the unconscious governs the individual, and since it is structured like language, the relationship between psychological manifestations—specifically attitudes and behavior associated with sex—and human biology is as arbitrary as the relationship between signifier and signified. Sex roles are just another cultural code, reducible to semiotics.

Lacan's stress on the phallus as a signifier—sublimation of it into the symbolic register—deconstructs the normative relationship between male/female and masculine/feminine. "It is the strength of the concept of the symbolic," says Jacqueline Rose, "that it systematically repudiates any account of sexuality which assumes the pre-given nature of sexual difference—the polemic within psychoanalysis and the challenge to any such 'nature' by feminism appear at their closest here."[35] But since the phallus is the mark of the individual's entry into personal identity, it is not just sexual identity that is problematized, but the nature of personhood itself; for the inevitable effect of the signifier (that is, the phallus) is to veil, to defer, to proclaim the absence of the signified. "In any case man cannot aim at being whole," Lacan maintains, "(the 'total personality' being another premise where modern psychotherapy goes off course) once the play of displacement and condensation, to which he is committed in the exercise of his functions, marks his relation as subject to the signifier."[36] According to Lacan, "Freud's most fundamental discovery [is] that the unconscious never ceases to challenge our apparent identity as subjects."[37] The very emergence of the conscious subject is precisely its *Spältung* or splitting from the unconscious, the realm of desire, which continues to motivate and govern the self, but which, by definition, it can never grasp or know: "The unconscious is that which, by speaking, determines the subject as being, but as a being to be crossed through with that metonymy by which I support desire, in so far as it is endlessly impossible to speak as such."[38] Hence the subject hopelessly seeks to define itself in relation to an object, the "Other," which is endlessly deferred by the process of signification, which is all that creates or "supposes" the subject in the first place: "The question of desire is that the fading subject yearns to find itself again by means of some sort of encounter with this miraculous thing defined by the phantasm."[39] In the Lacanian psychoanalytic economy, the identity of an individual is thus less substantial than the fantasies cast up by the formless desires that yield up such actuality as the "fading subject" can muster. This is an antihumanism indeed. The modern, Enlightenment drive to exalt humanity and render mankind divine has thus disintegrated into a postmodern "project" by which the very term *human* is rendered vacuous.

Lacan is after bigger game than mere human nature; his ultimate quarry is the same as Derrida's—God Himself. To be sure, like Bloom, Lacan sought to distance himself from deconstruction, and apparently his relations with Derrida were not good.[40] Nevertheless, like all the "uncanny" theorists who have become postmodernist pundits, Lacan influences literary study as an enemy of order and meaning—by his fear and loathing of the Logos. The concept of the "Other," he says, posited as "the place of speech, was a way, I can't say of laicising, but of exorcising our good old God"; and although he coyly declines the congratulations of those "many people who compliment me for having managed to establish...that God does not exist," "God" is only a "face" of the inaccessible "Other," as it is "supported by feminine *jouissance*"—a term meaning "bliss" or "enjoyment," but hinting at orgasm.[41] Such remarks explain why I have suggested that Lacan's feminist disciples are, metaphorically, crowning the phallic idol. Lacan deploys the notion of the phallus as signifier to reduce sexual differentiation to a mere splitting of human nature; it points towards the nameless emptiness of the "Other," which occupies the site of God and displaces the wisdom of the Logos with sheer absence: "This privilege of the Other thus sketches out the radical form of the gift of something which it does not have, namely, what is called its love."[42]

The implications for literary study of this vision of the human psyche are immense precisely because Lacan's peculiar form of atheism does not simply deny God, but instead confines him within psychoanalytic categories. Not "*God is dead*" but "*God is unconscious*" becomes "the true formula for atheism." As Jane Gallop remarks, "In place of the dead God, dead Father, Lacan offers us the unconscious father, unconscious, unaware, the father who does not know."[43] This formulation attacks God as Logos while leaving the name and notion intact, even as deconstruction employs the terms and concepts of metaphysics in order to dismantle it. A literary work infiltrated by Lacanian psychoanalysis is subjected to what might be oxymoronically termed "absolute relativism": whereas the old New Criticism would distinguish between the author's conscious purpose and the actual meaning of his work, maintaining that the former does not necessarily exhaust the latter, from Lacan's perspective there is no author, no intentional subject, to take into account. The author—that is, every source or principle of authority—is as "unconscious" as God, the originary source of all authority. Yet Lacan's subversion of authority *authorizes*, for example, Gallop's own treatment of the disobedience of Adam and Eve and their expulsion from the Garden of Eden in *Paradise Lost* as an encoded psychic drama of the emergence of the ego from the "mirror stage" into the uncertainty of the "symbolic order." According to Lacan, an infant becomes a "self" in the specular projection of his image, and acquires subjectivity by entering into the "symbolic order" of language. Just so Adam and Eve project their egos through disobedience and enter into the human condition with the Fall; as the infant discovers his inadequacy vis-à-vis the "Other," so Adam and Eve discover their nakedness.[44]

   The point is not that literary critics ought to be dissuaded from taking into account the insights and theories of psychoanalysis or other forms of psychology, although psychoanalytic interpretation is more persuasive when it heeds the cultural context of a literary work as well as the text itself. In any case, a critic is always free to contest the meaning of the poem with the poet. Lacan, however, has attacked the *author's* meaning by annihilating *meaning as such*. Literary meaning—along with every other kind—is displaced by an exploration of the psychic sources of the illusion that any meaning is possible. Here is Geoffrey H. Hartman with yet another weary dismissal of the notion that literary study has anything to do with interpreting works of literature:

> The emphasis has shifted from producing yet another interpretation, yet another exercise in casuistry, to understanding from within the institutional development of psychoanalysis, and from the inner development of Freud's writings, what kind of event in the history of interpretation psychoanalysis is proving to be.[45]

Evidently even psychoanalytic interpretation is interesting merely as an "event"—an historical phenomenon—although one might argue that determining "what kind of event" psychoanalysis is would itself qualify as a form of interpretation, or perhaps meta-interpetation.

An essay by Barbara Johnson in the same volume edited by Hartman, which recounts and comments on the quarrel between Lacan and Derrida over the *interpretation* of Poe's "The Purloined Letter," provides a fascinating spectacle of postmodernists condemning each other for the unforgivable heresy of deviating into sense. The rhetorical acrobatics on display in the effort to demonstrate that nothing can be demonstrated, that signification is an insignificant exercise, discloses a revealing picture of the contemporary academic circus. Johnson maintains that "'The Purloined Letter'...becomes for Lacan a kind of *allegory of the signifier*." As she sets forth the quarrel, Derrida faults Lacan for a regressively explicit explication of Poe's story; however, Derrida himself must descend into an equally fatal determinacy:

While asserting that the letter's meaning is lacking, Lacan, according to Derrida, makes this lack into *the* meaning of the letter. But Derrida does not stop there: he goes on to assert that what Lacan means by that lack is the truth of lack-as-castration-as-truth: "The truth of the purloined letter is the truth itself.... What is veiled/unveiled in this case is a hole, a nonbeing [*non-étant*]; the truth of being [*l'être*], as nonbeing. Truth is 'woman' as veiled/unveiled castration." Lacan himself, however, never uses the word "castration" in the text of the original seminar. That it is suggested is indisputable, but Derrida, by filling in what *Lacan* left blank, is repeating precisely the gesture of blank-filling for which he is criticizing Lacan.[46]

Johnson thus attempts to defend Lacan from the accusation of having presented a clear, definitive interpretation of a text by saying, in effect, *tu quoque*: you cannot say that Lacan has read an excessively stable meaning into Poe's text without yourself reading too much into Lacan's.

But Johnson can only make this argument by reading a great deal into both Lacan and Derrida: "And in fact, the more one works with Derrida's analysis, the more convinced one becomes that although the critique of what Derrida *calls* psychoanalysis is entirely justified, it does not quite apply to what Lacan's text is actually saying."[47] But if Johnson knows what Lacan's text is "actually saying," then she too must be "blank-filling," and not only in her treatment of Lacan, but also of Derrida, since she implicitly claims to know what Derrida is *actually saying about what Lacan is actually saying*. Of course, if any of these writers is *actually* saying anything at all, they are doing what deconstruction and Lacanian psychoanalysis both insist cannot *actually* be done. For the point of saying that "The

Purloined Letter" is "an allegory of the signifier" is that Poe never tells us the content of the letter, and its impact is wholly dependent on where it is in relation to the principal characters of the story— just as a signifier always defers the meaning of what is ostensibly signified and only has significance in its differential relation to other signifiers.

The quarrel could be summarized as follows: Lacan argues that Edgar Allen Poe's "The Purloined Letter" shows that a signifier functions without revealing meaning; Derrida maintains that Lacan has treated the non-meaning of the signifier as the meaning of the story and thus interpreted it as an integral discourse (i.e., as a logos), thereby slipping into logocentricism; and Johnson remarks that Derrida has misunderstood Lacan, whose view of signification is every bit as undecidable as Derrida's. Johnson thus joins the endless chase of the dog after its own tail. In the final words of her essay, she gives us as her final word that there can be no final word: "Far from giving us the seminar's final truth, these last words [of Lacan], and Derrida's readings of them, can only *enact* the impossibility of any ultimate analytical metalanguage, the eternal oscillation between unequivocal undecidability and ambiguous certainty."[48] What is going on here, at least in part, is a competition in obscurity: "Derrida dismisses Lacan's 'style' as a mere ornament," Johnson writes, "veiling, for a time, an unequivocal message: 'Lacan's "style," moreover, was such that for a long time it would hinder and delay all access to a *unique* content or a single unequivocal meaning determinable beyond the writing itself.'"[49] That is to say, Lacan's dense, elliptical style has led many readers to think him as much of a deconstructionist as Derrida, but Derrida himself has seen through Lacan, caught him attributing a single determinate meaning to a piece of writing—as if there were a distinction between language and meaning, between text and reality. In attempting to adjudicate the quarrel, Barbara Johnson implicitly claims to have the goods on both of them. It is as if a group of sleight-of-hand men were all claiming to know under which thimble the others had hidden their peas.

In this way, Derrida's deconstruction and its swirl of offshoots, emulators, and rivals—de Man's elegant despair, Bloom's energetic gnosticism, Lacan's revisionary psychoanalysis—all open the way for every kind of textual subversion and abuse. Deconstructionist assumptions, for example, provide the rationale for Johanna Smith's feminist reduction of Joseph Conrad's *Heart of Darkness* to a "complex interrelation of patriarchal and imperialist ideologies."[50] Similarly, Jacqueline Rose asserts that the current debate about psychoanalysis, with Lacan at its center, has taken on a "renewed urgency. Today, that urgency can be seen explicitly as political."[51] The psychoanalytic reduction of knowledge to desire opens into the "discourse of power" of the New Historicism, and this political twist marks another way that Lacanian psychoanalysis converges with deconstruction. Deconstruction can be seen as a distillation of the (il)logic of the postmodernist assault on Western culture. This assault, in all its manifestations, assumes a radical atheism, insofar as it decries the very concept of God as origin of order and meaning in the creation. Deconstruction is political, then, because it plays a role analogous to plastic explosives in the current campaign of terror against traditional academic norms of reason and civility. The common theme of the postmodern left, under all its various facades, is nihilism. Deconstruction, as a rationalistic method of undermining reason, is thus the choice "logic" of the fear and loathing of Logos.

CHAPTER FOUR

New Historicism: Literature and the Will to Power

The fundamental assumption of the "New Historicism," probably the most influential of the postmodern approaches to academic literary studies, is not in itself new. That man's life is driven by the engine of desire, and that this desire has profound political implications, are not novel ideas. Thomas Hobbes gives an especially blunt version of this viewpoint in *Leviathan*:

> ...the Felicity of this life, consisteth not in the repose of a mind satisfied. For there is no such *Finis ultimus*, (utmost ayme,) nor *Summum Bonum*, (greatest Good,) as is spoken of in the Books of the old Morall Philosophers. Nor can a man any more live, whose Desires are at an end, than he, whose Senses and Imaginations are at a stand. Felicity is a continuall progresse of the desire, from one object to another; the attaining of the former, being still but the way to the later.... So that in the first place, I put for a generall inclination of all mankind, a perpetuall and restlesse desire of Power after power, that ceaseth onely in Death.[1]

We find in Hobbes also a denigration of the specifically human integrity of the individual, which seems to anticipate the vitriolic antihumanism of much contemporary literary theory: "The *Value*, or WORTH of a man, is as of all other things, his Price; that is to say, so much as would be given for the use of his Power: and therefore is not absolute; but a thing dependant on the need and judgment of another."[2] What is new about the New Historicism is the way it applies such notions in literary study, since literature has traditionally been a principal source of our ideas of human dignity, and the way it subordinates works of literature to the historical process, understood in crudely materialistic terms.

The New Historicism, which undertakes an historical appropriation of literature, is both an adaptation of, and a reaction to, the models of "discourse theory" proffered by deconstruction and psychoanalysis. Although these postmodernist approaches are admirably suited to disrupting and decentering traditional Western metaphysical interpretation of reality and undermining the correlative moral conceptions of human nature, they are even more devastating when turned upon the various manifestations of secular ideology. Jacques Derrida, as we have seen in Chapter Two, is at his best in pointing out how supposedly materialistic, even atheistic, philosophies are covertly "logocentric." Traditional Western thought, especially Christianity, is far more resistant to deconstruction and psychoanalysis than "post-critical" humanisms. Classical humanism sees mankind afflicted with *hubris* and subject to fate, while Judaeo-Christian wisdom regards mankind as fallen and identifies pride as the chief of the deadly sins. Hence traditional thought can go a long way with deconstruction and psychoanalysis in acknowledging the *aporias* (or "hesitations" or "gaps") in our efforts to grasp the nature of things, the inadequacies in our means of signification, and, above all, the essential emptiness of the apparently autonomous, self-possessed human subject.

Now it is characteristic of the radical Left to sneer at all pieties save its own. The baby-boomers who occupied the offices of deans and professors during the campus revolutions of the Sixties are now occupying those same offices by the route of tenure and promotion; therefore, some basis was required to save the "ongoing revolution" from the *mise en abîme* of deconstruction and the toxic fumes of the discourse of the "Other" of Lacanian psychoanalysis. Since many of the most vocal and restless denizens of the contemporary academic world are enthralled by Marxist assumptions even when they do not actively profess Marxism, it is not at all surprising that "history" is the idol before which the great literary works of the Western tradition are to be sacrificed like so many garlanded heifers. Of course "history" is understood in a sense quite contrary to the usual conception: the study of the past is not intended to discover the order, purpose, and meaning underlying the chronicle of human events; rather, history is the disclosure of how human ideas of order, purpose, and meaning are all products of evolving conditions in the material environment. Works of literature, then, are merely documents, not essentially different from any other printed material, products of the economic and cultural hegemonies of their society. As such, literary works are no more "innocent" than other discourses; even the most personal lyric poem is implicated in the "discursive formations" of the regnant ideology. The task of the interpreter is to trace the ideological filiations and effects of such documents and show how they support repressive regimes and social practices (racism, sexism, imperialism, capitalism, and so on) and, more important, how literature can be used to undermine such "repression." For if literature is never innocent, neither is criticism; it is inevitably a practice of ideological reappropriation.

New Historicism is widely diffused among British and American literary scholars and assumes myriad forms, and there are different levels of ideological investment among those who make use of the analytic tools of New-Historicist practice. Still, a pervasive moral attitude and political inclination can be determined by singling out the most important contemporary intellectual influence as, yet another Frenchman, Michel Foucault. In a move reminiscent of Derrida and Lacan, Foucault sets out to invert the usual approach to the study of history: "It seems to me that the historical analysis of scientific discourse should, in the last resort, be subject, not to a theory of the knowing subject, but to a theory of discursive practice."[3] Foucault thus sets out to treat knowledge not as a voluntary attainment of the human mind but rather as a product of the "discursive practice" of a given era:

> What I am attempting to bring to light is the epistemological field, the *episteme* in which knowledge, envisaged apart from all criteria having reference to rational value or to its objective forms, grounds its positivity and thereby manifests a history which is not that of its growing perfection, but rather that of its conditions of possibility; in this account, what should appear are those configurations within the *space* of knowledge which have given rise to the diverse forms of empirical science. Such an enterprise is not so much a history, in the traditional meaning of that word, as an 'archaeology.'[4]

Archaeology deals with material artifacts; insofar as it treats the thought of an ancient culture, it does so as mediated by physical objects. To treat human knowledge as subject to "archaeology" rather than history in the traditional sense is to deprive knowledge of its intentionality or rationality. The implication is that knowledge is not the grasping and ordering of phenomena by the mind, but instead a phenomenon itself that produces the "mind"—mind, in turn, is thus theoretically reducible to the conditions of its production. Hence Foucault regards not only the mind but the very concept of human nature as a mere peculiarity of a certain period of "discursive formation": "It is comforting, however, and a source of profound relief to think that man is only a recent invention, a figure not yet two centuries old, a new wrinkle in our knowledge, and that he will disappear again as soon as that knowledge has discovered a new form."[5]

In a widely quoted essay, Foucault maintains that literary criticism once "constructed the figure of the author" in the same way that "Christian tradition authenticated (or rejected) the texts at its disposal."[6] Now, however, such questions as "How can a free subject penetrate the substance of things and give it meaning?" and "How can it activate the rules of language from within and thus give rise to the designs that are properly its own?" give way to the following:

> How, under what conditions, and in what forms can something like a subject appear in the order of discourse? What place can it occupy in each type of discourse, what functions can it assume, and by obeying what rules? In short, it is a matter of depriving the subject (or its substitute) of its role as originator, and of analyzing the subject as a variable and complex function of discourse.[7]

In this way Foucault argues that the author is an "ideological product," not, as Wordsworth would have it, "a man speaking to men."[8]

The implications of Foucault's notions of history for literary criticism are spelled out by Frank Lentricchia: "There is no essential, Platonic object—let us say a 'poem'—before which the discursive practice of literary criticism must (in its construction of a poetics and the methods of procedure that such a poetics would authorize) *make itself transparent.*"[9] Since all discursive practices, all orders of discourse, are ideologically motivated anyway, it is the business of the working critic to define and "valorize" literature in the interests of his own sociopolitical agenda.

The procedure is implicitly justified, in a loose fashion, on the grounds that the dominant culture, the reigning "hegemony," arbitrarily excludes any "discourse" that might challenge or threaten official discursive formations, or any that just seems different. To make the point, Lentricchia borrows from Foucault the example of the rejection of Gregor Mendel's genetic theories during the scientist's own lifetime, and adds the early failure of Robert Frost's poems. Mendel and Frost end up in very curious company:

> The cunning achievement of all such cultural systems is that they assign natural being to those inside their versions of truth and monsterhood to those outside. Robert Frost in the earlier phase of his career, Mendel, criminals, and the insane are alike monsters whose forced exclusion allows dominant cultural establishments to appropriate to themselves poetic truth, biological truth, rationality, sanity, social value, and well-being.[10]

This is quite a deft piece of sophistry. Our outrage is solicited against reigning scientific and cultural conventions because they have impeded the recognition of the genius of men like Mendel and Frost, although they were hardly treated like criminals or lunatics. But from the perspective of Foucault and Lentricchia, the incarceration of murderers and psychotics is in principle no different from the neglect of Mendel and Frost. Society is apparently no better equipped to establish norms of legality or sanity than to ascertain "poetic" or "biological" truth.

But neither is anyone else. The whole point of Foucault's concept of "discursive formation" is that it determines what members of any given community of discourse are able to "know." There is no "nature" or "truth" behind or beyond "discursive practice" that such practices represent with greater or lesser fidelity. And if there were, who would know, since our knowledge is the product of the practice it would have to judge? It is difficult to justify Lentricchia's outrage at cultural exclusions, for they seem an inescapable feature of "discursive practice"; however, the outrage is vehemently expressed, and it is not even mollified by repentance:

> The dramatic rise of both [Edward Arlington] Robinson and Frost after 1913 was not the result of a collective coming to good sense on the part of magazine editors, critics, contemporary poets, and other instruments of a repressive poetic discipline that had confined Robinson and Frost to speaking in a void. It is important to avoid sentimentality on this point. Strictly speaking, by Foucault's lights, Robinson and Frost were not liberated from incarceration by the modernist revolt; they were merely taken to new quarters of confinement, where under the authority of a different kind of repression their kinds of expression were granted the privilege of the poetic, even as other kinds were excluded and relegated to the status of the "old-fashioned."[11]

Lentriccia's anger and resentment, like Foucault's, are fueled by a sense of frustrated desire, by the realization that cultural norms mandate limitations on the expansiveness of the self. To be sure, he concedes that the integrated, intentional self is as problematic in Foucault as in Derrida: "To assert that the self is an 'empty synthesis' is to echo a key point of decentering: that the self is without ontological foundation." But Derrida's American disciples are wrong to place "the elements of synthesis into self-cancelling opposition, and in so doing effectively [to convert] history into a repetition of the

same by dissipating the force of changing historical determinates....
The self as synthesis is ontologically empty, but the consequence of
this insight need not be abysmal, for historically the self is a full
nexus of forces...."[12] Evidently, there are two realities in the world of
Foucault and Lentricchia, the forces generated by the surging of
historical processes and the force of desire—the urge to throw off
all restraints, to assert mastery, that possesses the illusory unity we call
a human consciousness.

Lentricchia effectively inverts the familiar meaning of "correct,"
which has always implied keeping to a straight line or rule. "The
readings of Derrida and Foucault are correct, then," Lentricchia says,
"not in some absolute sense, since they are powerless to totally
expunge logocentric passion from their own discourse, but because
they have acquired in their struggle with history a more intimate and
self-conscious grasp of the logocentric structures of constraint than
have any of the thinkers of their philosophical heritage."[13] Presumably Derrida and Foucault are "correct" in a *relative* sense—correct,
that is, insofar as they challenge the very notion of correctness entailed by the concept of the Logos. There is no sense that the
"logocentric" tradition is here assailed for the imposition of any
specific constraints—it is constraint itself, any constraint, that is to be
deplored. This is the predictable conclusion of Foucault's premises:
if there is no human nature to be maintained, if the "real" self is not
an integrated rational consciousness but only a nexus of desire and
historical necessity, then "constraint" can only seem an intolerable
burden.

Lentricchia himself supplies a remarkable sample of one variety
of New Historicist reading in a modern literary context. He begins
a twenty-five-page essay on Wallace Stevens' twelve-line poem,
"Anecdote of the Jar," by telling his own anecdote about an Italian
maternal grandfather. The punch line of the anecdote is in Italian,

and Lentricchia does not bother to translate much of it, some because it is too obscene, and the rest because the anecdote will not
be funny or comprehensible to us anyway, he says, because we lack
sufficient knowledge of his family and its circumstances forty odd
years ago. (I guess you had to be there.) In any case, in Lentricchia's
view, such is the fate of any anecdote; it requires a context because
it is supposed to be "a social form which instigates cultural memory:
the act of narrative renewal, the reinstatement of social cohesion....
If anecdotes had minds of their own they'd probably say, we don't
like modernist literary theories of aesthetic self-sufficiency; restore
us, good reader, to the way we were."[14] Now this is just the problem
posed by Stevens' "Anecdote": we have lost the social context of the
poem, and "modernist literary theories of aesthetic self-sufficiency"
merely produce a plethora of equivocal meanings and contradictory
readings—a point our critic spends more than ten pages illustrating.

Lentricchia sets out to solve the interpretive problem by
recontextualizing the poem—by putting it back in history. Michael
Herr, a Viet Nam war correspondent, alludes in passing to "Anecdote of the Jar" in his book *Dispatches* by comparing Khe Sanh to
"the planted jar in Wallace Stevens' poem." Stevens himself was a
student at Harvard when William James, noted professor of philosophy, was writing in the *Boston Transcript* to protest American intervention in the Philippines. Now Lentricchia eschews "a vulgar form
of historicism...in which the 'time' of the literary text is treated as
one and the same with political 'time,' as if the episode in the Philippines gave rise to the poem." The anti-imperialism of the poem,
written by a man generally regarded as a conservative Republican,
is purely a construction of the interpreter:

> Herr, Stevens, and James can be constellated as a single
> discursive body only because I've read them in a certain way;

I name the constellation, I give it a shape: "can be
constellated," a deluded construction; its passivity obscures
what goes on in the act of interpretation. So my hypotheticals
and subjunctives may be taken in another way, as an indication of where we always stand in the interpretive act: not
on the realist's terra firma but in active ideological contest
to shape our culture's sense of history. I offer Herr, Stevens,
and James (in that order, reading backward, which is always
the way reading takes place: through our cultural formation) as three voices from a tradition of American anti-im-
perialist writing (a unified cultural practice) that cuts through
the boundaries of philosophy, poetry, and journalism, a
discourse of political criticism.[15]

When interpretation is regarded as ideological expropriation, then
the meaning of a poem, of any text, is whatever serves the aims of
the ideologue. For Lentricchia, the *meaning* of "Anecdote of the Jar"
is the political screed that he manufactures out of a war
correspondent's casual allusion.

Ironically, it would be difficult to find a poem more at odds with
the fundamental premises of the New Historicism and of
postmodernist criticism in general. For what the jar suggests, above
all else, is man's capacity, through the construction and placement of
an artifact, to impose a center in what otherwise would appear to be
chaos. The jar placed by the poetic persona alters the appearance of
the natural world by giving it a structure and an orientation: "It made
the slovenly wilderness / Surround that hill."[16] Indeed, it *elevates* the
wilderness, and dispels its wildness, even though the wilderness still
sprawls: "The wilderness rose up to it, / And sprawled around, no
longer wild." The roundness of the jar is emphasized because of the
unlikelihood of finding any perfectly round object on the ground

of the Tennessee wilderness that is not man-made. It is "of a port in air" because it seems like something that might have dropped out of a portal or gateway in the sky. Perhaps a better oblique comment on the poem than Michael Herr's *Dispatches* is the South African film, *The Gods Must Be Crazy*, about the consternation among a tribe of Kalahari Desert Bushmen when one of them finds an intact soda bottle dropped by a passing airplane.

Lentricchia wishes to dismiss the art/nature dichotomy, perhaps because it is too facile, and concentrate instead on the derivation of *Tennessee* from *Tanasi*, the name of a Cherokee village, which recalls the displacement of the native inhabitants of North America by European settlers.[17] The facility of the art/nature motive, however, is the point of the poem, and Lentricchia is far more convincing when he brings in a parallel with Keats's "Ode on a Grecian Urn."[18] The wry twist in Stevens' "Anecdote" is that his jar is far colder and more alienated from nature than his Romantic predecessor's "Cold Pastoral":

It took dominion everywhere.
The Jar was gray and bare.
It did not give of bird or bush,
Like nothing else in Tennessee.

Like Keats's "Urn," Stevens' "Jar" is certainly designed to "tease us out of thought / As doth eternity"; but it does so with materials of considerably less sublimity. The humor in the poem results from this element of parody, but its import lies in the way it establishes a harmony of artistic awareness from generation to generation. The very fact that the twentieth-century poet can write a diminutive lyric that so unerringly recalls the grand ode of his Romantic forerunner and is yet so utterly different in tone points to an essential continuity in the human conception of art and life that

finally belies both deconstruction's "decentering" of literary meaning and the New Historicism's heedless political expropriation. It
is precisely in literature that something beyond the "desire for
power after power" is revealed in the human spirit. Lentricchia is
led astray by his New Historicist (or Marxist) assumptions: he
approaches "Anecdote of the Jar" as if it were a mere "document"
or "text" rather than a work of art—as if it were literally an anecdote
rather than an "anecdote," with the term used figuratively and
ironically. But of course "Anecdote of the Jar" is *literally* a poem:
that is, it is literally metaphorical, subsisting in the realm of analogy
and paradox.[19]

New Historicism may be said to have begun with Stephen
Greenblatt's *Renaissance Self-Fashioning*,[20] and the Renaissance has
remained a principal focus ever since. In *Chaste Thinking: The Rape
of Lucretia and the Birth of Humanism*, Stephanie Jed furnishes an especially striking example of the novel conception of history enter-
tained by many New Historicists. Jed produces 131 pages of critical
text on a Latin oration, *Declamatio Lucretiae* ("Lucretia's Declamation"),
written by Coluccio Salutati sometime around the turn of the fifteenth century, which occupies the back and front of ten leaves of
manuscript. According to the Roman historian Livy, the rape of the
respectable Roman matron by the dissolute son of King Tarquin,
provided the occasion for the expulsion of the royal house from
Rome and the establishment of the Republic under the leadership
of Junius Brutus. Salutati, a Florentine patriot as well as a humanist
scholar, linked the republican liberty of Florence with the ancient
Roman Republic, and Lucretia's accusation of Tarquin and justification of suicide to vindicate her honor was an obvious topic for a
rhetorical display piece.

Professor Jed, however, is too shrewd to be so easily taken in: "If
the narrative of Lucretia's rape somehow legitimizes the foundation

of Republican Rome, we might wonder if there is some kind of reciprocal relationship: do republican laws and institutions also legitimize the conditions of sexual violence?"[21] We are only a step away from a vast right-wing conspiracy. According to Jed's logic, Junius Brutus and his allies who expelled from Rome the monarchy that countenanced rape and the Florentine humanists who glorified this foundation of the Roman Republic are themselves deeply complicit in rape. Hence she writes of "a humanistic tradition that has celebrated Lucretia's rape as a prologue to republican freedom" and of "chastity as a cultural construct which invites sexual violence." In the *Declamatio* Salutati ascribes to Lucretia the notion that her reputation for chastity inspired Tarquin's lust, and this is evidence for Jed that it is chastity, not Tarquin's twisted arrogance, which leads to the rape: "In this way, she is inscribed in a language that invites sexual violence."[22] Jed's radical feminist response to "blaming the victim" is thus to blame the defenders of the victim.

The argument becomes still more contrived as Jed links philological practices of humanist "ideology" to what she regards as the Roman Republic's preoccupation with chastity on the basis of the word *castigare*, which applies both to Junius Brutus' "chastising" of the Tarquin kings and, subsequently, of his own rebellious sons, and also to the humanist's efforts to purify classical texts from "contamination" by scribal errors.[23] Both are examples of what she calls "chaste thinking." To be sure, Jed concedes that "chaste thinking" does not refer "to any historical truth about Florence in the fifteenth century" and that "the figure of chaste thinking is nowhere explicitly articulated in humanistic texts."[24] But Jed is all too typical of much New Historicist writing insofar as she is less interested in history than in herself:

> Moreover, without such evidence as I have mustered here, linking Florentine concepts of liberty both to the legends

of Lucretia's rape and Brutus' castigating behavior and to the
humanists' replication of these narratives in their violation
and castigation of Roman texts, I would still feel cut off from
a tradition which has persistently celebrated the rape of
Lucretia as a prologue to republican freedom. Only in the
process of documenting the representation of the humanists' contact with Roman texts, and the role this contact played
in the generation of political thought, have new interpretive
possibilities emerged which begin to include me as a reader
and writer about humanism.[25]

The implication of remarks such as these is Jed's determination to
appropriate not only Salutati's *Declamatio Lucretiae* but the entire
institution of historical literary criticism to a feminist political
agenda and the gratification of her own obscure personal needs.
She attacks not merely a particular humanist work or author, or
even a particular flaw in humanist practice, but the whole humanist
"ideology"; that is, the commitment to disinterested scholarship in
the service of objective truth. She thus seeks to subvert the
fundamental concept of liberal education, of which a principal aim
is to cultivate a faculty of critical inquiry and a spirit of dispassionate
impartiality.

Jed's argument depends upon a set of crudely materialistic assumptions. If a work of literature exists only as ink marks on paper,
if there is no intentional structure of meaning that transcends these
material components, then the chief humanist legacy to modern
scholarship—the application of textual criticism to restore the integrity of works corrupted by scribal errors, interpolations, and the
like—is simply pointless:

> When a philologist "castigates" a text by injecting names
> and spellings that are foreign to the tradition of the text being

edited, that text is contaminated by the intervention of the philologist. Even if the readings supplied by the philologist are more "correct" than those supplied by the text's own tradition, the "castigation" of a text means the demise of its integrity. Intending to restore a text to its integrity or to a state prior to its having been touched and thereby contaminated by human hands, the philologist only contributes to the text's ulterior contamination. A text made chaste or castigated by a philologist is, by definition, a contaminated text, a text that has suffered the wounds of being handled or touched. Philological thought, from that of the early humanists to that of modern scholars of humanism, has tended to obscure the history and politics of this contradiction, even though, as heirs to philological practice, we are always reproducing it.[26]

The sophistry here is to treat "text" as if it meant merely a particular manuscript or other physical "witness" of a text, but this usage depends upon accepting as a given the deconstructive premise that there is "nothing outside of the text"; that is, since there is no determinate relationship between signifier and signified, we can never know what a writer *meant*, only what he—or a copyist—*wrote*. If this premise is accepted and applied logically, then one could never with confidence correct a typographical error, and the judicious philologist and the careless scribe would become indistinguishable.[27]

Now it is certainly true that meaning is elusive and sometimes irrecoverable, and that textual editors—like the copyists whom they "castigate"—make errors; but this does not mean that the actual significance of a work can never be ferreted out of a faulty textual tradition. As Guy Lee points out, in *all* the surviving manuscripts on which the text of Virgil's *Eclogues* depended, the last half of line 107 of Eclogue VIII had read, "et Hylas in limine latrat" ("and Hylas is barking in the doorway"). Then it occurred to someone in the fifteenth century that Virgil must have written—or intended to write—not *Hylas* (a common masculine name in pastoral poetry), but *Hylax* (Greek for "Barker," the equivalent of "Fido" or "Spot"); and no one has challenged the emendation since, because it is self-evidently correct despite the lack of manuscript support. As Lee observes, this unanimity of interpretation is "a good example of the certainty attainable in literary studies, which ignorant fashion nowadays regards as incurably subjective."[28] While there will always be room for debate about obscure passages and need for refinement of interpretive nuances, a general consensus is certainly possible about the general meaning of the great works of literature in the Western tradition. The source of consternation for many New Historicists and other postmodernists is that most great works are great precisely because they provide a powerful alternative to the moral relativism and materialism typical of so many contemporary academics.

The most compelling realization of the unique dignity of mankind, which is the foundation for traditional religion and morality, is furnished by those authors who have long been recognized for surpassing excellence. In the English-speaking world Shakespeare holds pride of place, and this doubtless accounts for the almost frenzied activity on the part of New Historicists to diminish the power of Shakespearean drama or to assimilate it to the ideological program of the radical Left. A volume of essays collected from the 1986 International Shakespeare Conference held in (of all places) West Berlin, while the Wall still stood, furnishes an illuminating example of the New Historicism at work. The editors of the volume, Jean Howard and Marion O'Connor, would doubtless reprove my blanket use of the term, since their "Introduction" treats "new historicism" as one of "several contemporary developments" along with "feminism" and "various forms of Marxist criticism, including cultural materialism." Nevertheless, even they point out that these supposedly diverse strands often converge:

> At the same time, it is the twin pressures of historicism and materialism which most radically are altering American feminist criticism. The necessity to historicize gender constructions if one wishes to escape the oppressive notion of a universal human nature, or, worse, of an eternal feminine, is increasingly apparent, as is the need to talk about the way race and class affect constructions of the feminine and pluralize the monolithic concept of "woman."[29]

I need only add that just as the feminists are increasingly succumbing to "the twin pressures of historicism and materialism," even so one would be hard-pressed to find an historicist who is not also a materialist and a feminist, or a materialist who is not also a feminist and an historicist. They all agree in their loathing for "the oppressive notion of a universal human nature," and this is more significant than any local disagreements. The editors themselves also point out a certain homogeneity in the backgrounds of their authors: "Most of the contributors, having been students at North American universities in the 1960s and in the early years of academic employment in the 1970s, have been constructed by discourses both theoretical and political." The "tensions and contradictions among these discourses" notwithstanding, the book "voices the desire to change—if not the world—at least the academy."[30] In other words, since these folk have all been "constructed" by the same small circle of discursive contractors—like so many suburban tract houses—we may expect a certain similarity in the floor plans.

The ruthless politicizing of literary scholarship and of higher education in general is blatantly evident in the introductory essay, which sets out "to further a political analysis of Shakespearean texts and their uses in culture." The editors' basic premise recalls Foucault and Lentricchia: "that reality is knowable only through the discourses which mediate it, and that there is a constant, if subterranean, struggle over whose constructions of the real will gain dominance." Any staging, reading, critical interpretation, or pedagogical presentation of a play by Shakespeare (or anyone else for that matter) is a "construction" of the play and therefore a power move in the game of cultural politics: "There is...no way to place a drama outside of ideological contestation, ideology being understood as that inescapable network of beliefs and practices by which variously positioned and historically constituted subjects imagine their relationship to the real and through which they render intelligible the world around them."[31] The pedagogical implications of such nihilism are alarming: liberal education is reduced once again to sophistry—to a "contestation" over the shape of the shadows on the wall in Plato's cave.[32]

It is crucial to realize that Howard and O'Connor are not saying that self-interest and self-aggrandizement are an inevitable (if regrettable) *factor* in the creation, interpretation, and presentation of works of art; rather, they are saying that nothing is outside of ideology, which constructs not only each and every self, but even the very idea of a "self." Citing Louis Althusser, they maintain that, "Ideology can never be 'disinterested' because it functions to render 'obvious' and 'natural' constructions of reality which, often in oblique and highly mediated ways, serve the interests of particular races, genders and classes within the social formation." In describing the diverse ideological ramifications of Shakespearean drama, the critic is not seeking an essential Shakespeare that exists apart from politics: "Far from distorting the 'true' meaning of an unchanging text, however, such constructions *are* the text: it lives in history, with history itself understood as the field of contestation." Having thus undermined any conceivable basis for choosing among these competing "ideologies"—that is, any rational basis, anything beyond raw desire or blasé velleity—Howard and O'Connor then proceed to extol intensity of commitment: "A further aim of much political criticism, however, is not only to *describe*, but to *take a position on*, the political uses of texts: to challenge some critical, theatrical, or pedagogical practices involving Shakespeare and to encourage others."[33] Perhaps the theoretical source for the ferocious hostility of the champions of political correctness is here displayed: since their strictures and precepts have no basis in rational principle or argument, any objection can only be taken personally.

"We go to great writers for the truth," wrote John F. Danby five decades ago at the beginning of a study of *King Lear.* "Or for whatever reason we go to them in the first place it is for the truth we return to them, again and again."[34] Anyone who ventured such a statement in an academic forum today would probably provoke derision among the trendier part of his audience and acute embarrassment among most of the rest. To such an extent has the very idea of truth existing independently of our "ideological constructions" been banished from the universities founded for the purpose of discovering and promulgating the truth. (Reflect upon the irony that *Lux et veritas* is the motto of Yale University.) Howard and O'Connor dismiss the kind of interpretation undertaken by Danby simply by reciting the mantra "History":

> Accompanying the contention that Shakespeare depicts a universal and unchanging human nature are often two further claims: first, that the meaning of a Shakespearean text is ineluctably *in* that text (and consequently never changes);

and second, that the Shakespearean text resides in an aesthetic zone above ideology. One stark link among these
claims is their avoidance of history. To posit an unchanging
meaning *in* texts, waiting to be found by "good" readers, is
to deny the historicity of the reading and theatrical practices
through which a plural and opaque text is rendered intelligible at different historical moments and from different
interested positions within the social formation.[35]

The argument is, again, based on the sophistry of shifting the
meaning of a term: "history" in this quotation does not mean a
knowledge of the relationship between works of literature and the
various historical circumstances in which they were written. Such
objective knowledge is impossible for the prisoners of the regnant
"social formation." "History," for Howard and O'Connor, is just
another ideological construct, which here means accepting without
question—as a self-evident *truth*—that a work of literature is *only* an
historical "construction" whose identity "alters when it alteration
finds" in historical conditions. It means, in other words, "privileging" the Marxist, materialist view that history must be "understood
as a field of contestation." To deny categorically that truth exists
apart from "ideological constructions" is, of course, to claim that
one of these constructions—the one favored by New Historicism
—is "true."

It is important to recognize that the New Historicism is not merely
an abstract intellectual venture; its adherents have serious political
designs on the control of higher education. "It is only too easy to
read and/or write as a born-again poststructuralist/Marxist and still
teach like an unregenerate New Critic," Howard and O'Connor
complain.[36] They offer suggestions that make plain how a New
Historicist pedagogy would alter the entire conception of a class in
literature in explicitly political terms:

A course that attempts in this way to talk about plays in history and ideology will not "cover" the usual array of literary texts. It will, instead, be investigating a range of social texts and practices against which to assess, differentially, the specific function of the theater and of dramatic representations, and it will be preoccupied with theorizing the ground of its own undertaking. In both regards it will be offering a counterpractice to those usually predominating in the teaching of Shakespeare.[37]

There is, to be sure, the worry that an assistant professor who attempts such a course could have difficulty with tenure and promotion: "In a department where 'Shakespeare' is a required course and most sections of the course cover thirteen plays a semester, will an instructor who teaches only three plays and an array of theoretical and nondramatic Renaissance texts, be judged as having taught Shakespeare 'well,' no matter what rationale he or she offers for this mode of approaching the course?"[38] Once we have found a department that still requires "Shakespeare," the question ought to be, has this "born-again poststructuralist/Marxist" taught *Shakespeare* at all. For such an "approach" to the "course" amounts to a redefinition not only of Shakespearean drama, but of literary education in general. "The array of theoretical and nondramatic Renaissance texts" will ensure that the three plays allotted to Shakespeare will not be allowed to speak in the poet's authentic voice, but will be diluted by the ideological preoccupations and biases of the instructor. An alert student who is exposed to a dozen or more plays by Shakespeare in a semester will be caught up in his powerful dramatic vision, and the quirks of his professor—whether the latter is liberal or conservative, communist or capitalist, old or young—will matter less. But Howard and

O'Connor wish to have Shakespeare's voice muted and to suppress the idea that he presents a unique insight into human experience that transcends the milieu of "an Elizabethan tract railing against crossdressing" and "a stage on which male actors routinely impersonate women."[39] In any case, the fears of Howard and O'Connor for the career prospects of the Marxist innovator are largely unfounded. The administrators of most American colleges and universities nowadays have the mentality of entertainment executives, and to call oneself "experimental" or "interdisciplinary," which sounds like a good marketing strategy, is a virtual guarantee of tenure and promotion.

A startling indication of the aims of the New Historicism and its utter disregard for the traditional concerns of literary study, as well as its contempt for Western culture, is provided by Thomas Cartelli in "Prospero in Africa: *The Tempest* as colonialist text and pretext," one of the essays in the Howard/O'Connor collection. Cartelli hardly discusses *The Tempest* as such—after all, according to his materialist perspective, *The Tempest* as such can hardly be said to exist. The "construction" of it he presents is largely derived from *A Grain of Wheat* (1967) by the Nigerian novelist Ngugi Wa Thiong'o, with additional comments by other black Third World writers. In the novel Ngugi "has a brutal but (in his own eyes) 'well-meaning' British colonial functionary plan to write a book on his experiences in Kenya entitled 'Prospero in Africa.'"[40] The functionary, having met and been impressed by a number of British-educated Africans, becomes a believer in the ideals of fraternity and equality and decides to devote his life to bringing civilization to as many Africans as possible. The Mau Mau rebellion, however, brings bitter disillusionment, which "leads ultimately not to a book, but to an official investigation of his role in the deaths of eleven prisoners in the concentration camp over which he came to preside."[41] Like Kurtz in Conrad's *Heart of Dark-*

ness, Ngugi's British colonialist moves from benevolent idealism to genocidal atrocities.

Cartelli endorses what he calls Ngugi's "ideological position...a position that reads into Prospero's dispossession of Caliban the entire history of the destruction of African culture."[42] Ngugi is apparently uninterested in a more subtle reading of *The Tempest*, since it would get in the way of political activism: "Shakespeare's attitude toward Prospero is no more his point than is Conrad's similarly complex attitude toward Kurtz. Given Ngugi's position as a politically committed African writer, *The Tempest*'s historical distance from *Heart of Darkness* is insignificant, Prospero's difference from Kurtz negligible, insofar as each participates in a common colonialist enterprise that has seldom been known to make distinctions between its colonized subjects."[43] One of the leading features of Western civilization—especially in the arts—is precisely the capacity to make distinctions; but this feature, because it sometimes fails, is rejected by Ngugi along with such injustices as European colonists perpetrated against the native populations of their colonies. Western virtues are to be rejected along with the vices, and Cartelli, a literature professor in an American college, refuses, on account of his New Historicist ideology, to defend *The Tempest* as a work of art that transcends whatever ideological uses it may have suffered at the hands of imperialism:

> For Ngugi, a historically or critically "correct" reading of *The Tempest* that isolates the play "at its originating moment of production" would serve merely an antiquarian's interest, documenting an alleged "intervention" in colonialist discourse that made no discernibly positive impact on the subsequent development of colonial practices. His own variety of historicity would, on the other hand, focus on all that has intervened between the text's originating moment

and the present moment of reception; it would thus focus less on the text's status as a historically determined literary artifact, now open to a variety of interpretations, than on its subordination to what history has made of it.[44]

If literature's entire existence is ideological, then its only value will be as propaganda; and if the "other side" has preempted a particular play, then it must be depreciated. Because "the text of *The Tempest* continues to allow Prospero the privilege of the grand closing gesture; continues to privilege that gesture's ambiguity at the expense of Caliban's dispossession," Cartelli concludes, "...*The Tempest* is not only complicit in the history of its successive misreadings, but responsible in some measure for the development of the ways in which it is read."[45]

Now there is a great deal of nonsense here (how can a "text," which only exists as it is "constructed" by various ideological determined readings, be "responsible" for anything?), but what I wish to draw attention to is the way the moral polarity of Prospero and Caliban has been reversed. In the fiction of the play, Caliban is a literal monster, offspring of a demon and a witch, with scales like a fish. Still, he is treated well by Prospero until he attempts to rape the magician's young daughter, Miranda, a deed for which he remains impenitent until the end of the play. Only after the attempted rape does Prospero confine him and force him to labor. It seems clear that Caliban and his spiritual counterpart Ariel are, in the words of the Oxford Shakespeare, "two of Shakepeare's most obviously symbolic characters."[46] Caliban is a symbol for the intractable and brutish element in fallen human nature, and one can well understand the natives of former colonies bitterly resenting their association with Caliban by Europeans. If Cartelli's understanding is correct, however, Ngugi and his *confrères* willingly accept the identification with Caliban, and

Cartelli seems not at all troubled by this. Prospero's horror at the attempted rape is apparently just cultural imperialism, and presumably efforts of European colonists to suppress such native customs as cannibalism and human sacrifice are equally ethnocentric. It is especially ironic that Cartelli, who doubtless bears impeccable feminist credentials, finds it impossible to condemn rape wholeheartedly, not at least if the rape is attempted by a character taken to represent Third World natives.

Cartelli is not the only academic entangled in the moral contradictions of political correctness. Kim Hall, an African American woman, who claims to be a feminist, concedes that "Caliban's response [*Tempest* I.ii.351-53] indicates that he did indeed make advances to Miranda"[47]—although "made advances" seems a rather tame euphemism. Nevertheless, Prospero, who is treated as a combination of Cecil Rhodes and night-riding Klansman, is allowed no genuine concern about his daughter's safety and honor: "It is in response to Caliban's claim of property rights that Prospero charges Caliban with rape, a rhetorical move that reinforces Valerie Smith's point that 'instances of interracial rape constitute sites of struggle between black and white men that allow privileged white men to exercise property rights over the bodies of white women.'"[48] By the same token, since Ferdinand obviously desires Miranda sexually, he and Caliban share a "basic sexuality" and are not significantly different: "These similarities in some ways suggest that the 'real' difference between Caliban and Ferdinand is racial, not moral or sexual."[49]

Both Cartelli and Hall are grossly patronizing to the men of former European colonies, because they imply that uncivilized customs and behavior are an integral part of their nature and identity, not the remnants of past ages that have remained among them longer than among Europeans because of historical contingencies. One of the truly curious aspects of the New Historicism is how uninterested so many of its practitioners are in the actual history of evolving cultures. Indeed anything that could reasonably be called "history"— an endeavor at a rational comprehension of human development through time—is foreclosed by relativism and materialism. Since what counts as civilized behavior is a matter of ideological construction, it is difficult to determine on what basis any individual or regime could be approved or condemned—Shakespeare or Prospero, Stalinism or Nazism.

Such outright denigration of Shakespeare as Cartelli and Hall exhibit is not yet the usual mode of "political criticism," although it will probably grow more common. The typical approach now is to recruit Shakespearean drama for the promulgation of the leftist ideological program of choice. Thus Stephen Greenblatt, the doyen of American New Historicists, sets about to undermine traditional norms of sexual identity and conduct by archly calling our attention to the fact that women's roles were played by boys on the Elizabethan stage. He proceeds to illuminate *Twelfth Night* by invoking a contemporaneous French case involving a youth of hermaphroditic traits who, though reared as a girl, wished to be, and turned out to be, predominantly male upon reaching maturity. From this curious incident, which would now be the stuff of tabloid television, Greenblatt furnishes us with solemn platitudes: "The concrete individual exists only in relation to forces that pull against spontaneous singularity and that draw any given life, however peculiarly formed, toward communal forms."[50] Now it is hard to see why Greenblatt would even attempt to take this story from France as evidence for the usual feminist and New Historicist proposition that "gender" is "socially constructed," since the youth in question risked being burned alive for a crime against nature in order to assert his essential and natural masculinity. But in fact Greenblatt uses the anecdote as historical background for this reading of Shakespeare's comedy:

"Though by divine and human decree the consummation of desire could be licitly figured only in the love of a man and a woman, it did not follow that desire was inherently heterosexual. The delicious confusions of *Twelfth Night* depend upon the mobility of desire." For Greenblatt, an historical contingency—that women were not permitted to perform publicly in the Elizabethan theatre—becomes central to the meaning of *Twelfth Night*: "The open secret of identity—that within differentiated individuals is a single structure, identifiably male—is presented literally in the all-male cast."[51] Here the scholar is so entangled in the crude details of historicist materialism that he fails to acknowledge the triumph of Shakespeare's art. In the character of Viola, a boy playing a girl disguised as a boy furnishes a luminous dramatization of feminine nature (of the "eternal feminine," one is tempted to say). It is difficult to imagine a more decisive, concrete refutation of the premises of the New Historicism: in the face of seemingly insuperable material circumstances (no women allowed on stage), Shakespeare's dramas present a gallery of women characters whose femininity ought to be the envy of Hollywood starlets.

An essay on *King Lear* by David Aers and Gunther Kress, which treats the play as an allegory of the Marxist dialectic of history, provides another example of ideological blindness. Lear, Gloucester, and Kent represent the traditional feudal order as it is challenged and overthrown by nascent capitalism embodied in the persons of Goneril, Regan, Cornwall, and, above all, Edmund. Consider, for example, their comment on Edmund's bribing of a "Captain" to murder Lear and Cordelia:

> The exchange between the two exemplifies the new ethos in action. Edmund appeals to no personal loyalties, traditional values or fixed obligations. Instead he accepts social

mobility and market relations as the reality within which "employment" is bestowed: men's labour and obedience is [*sic*] to be *bought* for particular services, and men who sell their labours to an employer in this way, and wish for continued "employment" from him, will be "as the time is," in the current employer's definition. All consideration of human ends, of moral or social values, is dissolved as the employee accepts a highly abstract definition of "man's work," one which is appropriate to the new social organization and relationships.[52]

But Aers and Kress find little that is good to match the evil in *King Lear*. Cornwall's servant who kills his master and loses his own life in an effort to prevent him from blinding Gloucester "acts out of a belief in the older values"; but apparently his action is morally (as well as practically) futile: "Cordelia recognizes that in the society of *King Lear* the relation between meaning and symbol has broken down; the servant does not, and wishes to protect his master Cornwall from carrying out an action which he feels Cornwall would not wish to commit."[53] Evidently these critics regard an ineffectual action—an action that fails to heed the breakdown "between meaning and symbol"—as *meaningless*, no matter how good its intention. One way of establishing the moral orientation of a literary interpreter is to find out whether he deems this nameless servant, who appears in only one scene and loses his own life in a vain effort to save an old man's eyes, a hero or a hapless victim of history.

Aers and Kress are less crude than older generations of Marxist literary critics, who treat Cordelia and her supporters as harbingers of the Marxist "classless society." Aers and Kress do observe that "in her relations with those characters who are important to her, Kent and Lear, she uses the direct, personal language." They also note, however, that while Cordelia says "thou" to Kent, he still addresses her with the formal "you." The playwright, they concede, is no egalitarian: "Shakespeare is not attacking the traditional language and the inherited social form as such, but is attacking its debased version, where it has lost value and significance, and is used merely as a cynical device by those who hold a quite different ideology." They also suspect that "Shakespeare felt a nostalgia for the traditional order he presented both critically and in a process of disintegration," and evidently all that saves the play is that "the last two lines...convey a wholly negative effect." Although their view is far more affirmative than Cartelli's or Hall's, they still regard Shakespeare as a prisoner of his historical era, unable to foresee the glories of the Marxist utopia: "In our view, the tension here comes from Shakespeare's inability to imagine any real alternative beyond the disintegrating traditional order and the utterly destructive individualism which emerges from it."[54]

In such a treatment of *King Lear*, we confront the full inadequacy of "political criticism." At the end of the fourth act, after a night of mad raving in a storm on the desolate heath, the dispossessed Lear awakens to find himself in the presence of his banished daughter who has risked everything—and will lose it all—to return and save him from her sisters:

Lear: Be your tears wet? Yes, faith. I pray, weep not.
         If you have poison for me, I will drink it.
         I know you do not love me; for your sisters
         Have, as I do remember, done me wrong.
         You have some cause; they have not.

Cordelia: No cause, no cause. (IV.vi.64-69)

Surely this is among the finest dramatizations of Christian charity and forgiveness in the English language—an exquisite expression of the graciousness, indeed of the grace, without which political arrangements of any kind are doomed to end in ignominy and violence. In the face of moments such as these in *King Lear*, Aers and Kress are content to wonder whether Cordelia is conscious of the "inevitably skewed relationship," the "unbridgeable gulf" between "the powerful" and the "(relatively) less powerful."[55]

It is troubling to think that Shakespeare, along with many other great poets, is routinely presented to American college students as a running dog of imperialism, or a sexist pig, or, at best, a nostalgic conservative, who failed to grasp the superior political wisdom of cultural materialism. It is comforting, on the other hand, to realize that Shakespeare's work will outlast the New Historicism and other such "ideological constructions." The salvation of literature will be effected, finally, by the inherent value of literary works themselves.

CHAPTER FIVE

Constitutional Interpretation and Literary Theory

It would be comforting to assume that the New Historicism, cultural materialism, and other forms of "political criticism" were literally of merely "academic" interest; however, thoughtful men and women will quickly acknowledge the crucial influence of higher education on the cultural and political health of a nation. The scholarly community plays a major role in defining the terms in which debate is conducted and in shaping the imaginative horizons not only of students, but even of the general public. The lucubrations of professors, no matter how improbable or obscure, have a way of infiltrating the decision-making process of various public institutions and even businesses as well as the several branches of government. Controversy during the last two decades over the interpretation of the United States Constitution by the federal courts has brought to light a fateful convergence of judicial practice and academic theory. The similarity between the aims and assumptions of postmodernist literary theory and the approach of "judicial activists" to constitutional interpretation reveals a strikingly consistent hostility of leftists from various professional fields to the moral and intellectual traditions of Western civilization, and it provides an admonition to the prudent that the "merely academic" business of liberal education must not be neglected.

Interpretation became a high profile political issue in the election campaigns of 1980 and 1984, when the appointment of "strict constructionists" to the Supreme Court was an important plank in the Republican Party platform and a major promise of candidate Ronald Reagan. Hence when Attorney General Edwin Meese, in a 1985 speech to the American Bar Association, explained the administration's policy of seeking to appoint men and women to the federal bench who would interpret the Constitution in the light of the "original intention" of its framers, he was hardly breaking new ground. By the autumn of that year, however, Meese's speech had drawn a remarkably acerbic response from a sitting Supreme Court justice. Without mentioning the Attorney General by name, Justice William Brennan derided as "facile historicism" Meese's call for federal judges to return to the original meaning of the Constitution and condemned as "arrogance clothed as humility" the effort to "gauge accurately the intent of the Framers." Brennan's outrage was soon echoed by another Supreme Court justice, John Paul Stevens, as well as by a predictable band of professors and editorialists.[1] Now the significance of Meese's public campaign for traditional interpretation of the Constitution, which continued for more than a year,[2] transcends the usual political sideshow in the media because of the reaction it provoked from sitting justices. As Raoul Berger observed, "For the first time a justice of the Supreme Court...has openly laid claim to judicial power to revise the Constitution."[3]

Meese of course enjoyed the support of numerous distinguished commentators—in addition to Berger—whose views appeared in a variety of syndicated columns and journal articles. In fact, the Meese position seems almost too self-evident: surely the Constitution should be interpreted in accordance with the intentions of the men who wrote it? Surely the meaning of any document lies in the meaning of the words on the page and not in the biases or whims of the interpreter? At the time of the skirmishes occasioned by Edwin Meese's foray into enemy-occupied judicial territory, it was tempting to see the aberrant federal court decisions of recent years as the singular work of a clique of perversely maverick judges appointed by liberal Democrats. Even the disappointing performance of many Nixon, Reagan, and Bush appointees allowed numerous commentators to regard the problem as peculiar to the judicial system, which had somehow drifted away from the common sense and common rational standards of the learned world as a whole. Thus Joseph Sobran, with poignantly impatient frustration, underscores the eccentricity and irresponsibility of Justice Brennan's mode of constitutional interpretation by contrasting it to strict standards of literary criticism:

When I was a literature student in college, it was always stressed that the first thing you had to know about a text was what the words meant in their own time. Nobody cared what sublime emotions or fantasies the poet's words stirred in your own breast. The job of the scholar was to discover meaning, not to invent it or impose it.... Liberal scholars want to apply to the Constitution a method of understanding they would flunk any undergraduate for applying to Chaucer or Milton. If you buy a pocket edition of John Donne's poetry, you will find it full of footnotes that instruct you in what some of the words meant in Donne's time. The editor will definitely not tell you that it's up to you to apply Donne's words as you see fit to contemporary situations, and never mind what those words meant to the poet and his audience.

Any scholar who said anything so fatuous would give his professional reputation a severe wound.[4]

Sobran, who was evidently taught by New Critics and old-fashioned historical scholars, articulates the voice of exasperated common sense: what could be simpler than to silence Justice Brennan merely by appealing to the normal practices of college literature professors? Regrettably, the academic literary community, as the first four chapters of this book have shown, can hardly be counted on to provide support against the vagaries of judicial interpretation. The interpretive approaches deprecated by Sobran as undergraduate follies are now quite often winning moves in the race for tenure, promotion, and professional standing. By the time Meese and Sobran had entered the lists on behalf of common sense in constitutional interpretation, Catherine Belsey's *Critical Practice*, which appeared in Methuen's *New Accents* series of brief handbooks designed to inform students about—and indoctrinate them in—the latest trends in critical theory, was about to go into a fourth printing. The first chapter devotes more than thirty pages to disparaging common sense and concludes that the revolution has not gone far enough:

> To liberate new ways of reading which overcome the theoretical problems and the practical limitations I have discussed in this necessarily selective account of some of the available theories, we need a new theoretical framework which makes a fundamental break with the propositions of common sense. The assaults on expressive realism I have sketched do not constitute such a break. Post-Saussurean linguistics, however, undermines common sense in a more radical way and so provides a theoretical framework which permits the development of a genuinely radical critical practice.[5]

G. K. Chesterton could have predicted the results of this unnatural coupling of literary theory and continental linguistic philosophy: "Since the modern world began in the sixteenth century, nobody's system of philosophy has really corresponded to everybody's sense of reality; to what, if left to themselves, common men would call common sense." What Chesterton says about the "modern philosopher" applies even more forcefully to the postmodern theorist: "The modern philosopher claims, like a sort of confidence man, that if once we will grant him this, the rest will be easy; he will straighten out the world, if once he is allowed to give this one twist to the mind."[6] The principal difference is that the postmodernist has abandoned even the pretense of straightening things out and is committed to nothing but twistedness.

Outrageous and deplorable judicial decisions—*Roe v. Wade* and its sequelae, for instance—are not simply the result of distortions of our judicial system; rather, they are reflections of a culture that is intellectually and morally decadent in its highest and lowest reaches. The humanities cannot be called in to check the oxymoronically antinomian tendencies of jurisprudence, because the humanities themselves, metamorphosing from "humane letters" into "human sciences," have become antihumanist and even antihuman, even as the law has become lawless. According to Geoffrey Hartman, it has long been the consensus of literary critics and scholars that "literary humanism was dead."[7] *The Abolition of Man*, C. S. Lewis' slender 1947 volume on the condition of education in our century, has proven chillingly prophetic. Catherine Belsey's attack on common sense enfolds an underlying attack on the bearer of common sense, mankind. As we have seen, this view receives its characteristic formulation by Michel Foucault:

> Strangely enough, man—the study of whom is supposed by the naïve to be the oldest investigation since Socrates—is

probably no more than a kind of rift in the order of things, or, in any case, a configuration whose outlines are determined by the new position he has so recently taken up in the field of knowledge. Whence all the chimeras of the new humanisms, all the facile solutions of an "anthropology" understood as a universal reflection on man, half-empirical, half-philosophical. It is comforting, however, and a source of profound relief to think that man is only a recent invention, a figure not yet two centuries old, a new wrinkle in our knowledge, and that he will disappear again as soon as that knowledge has discovered a new form.[8]

One might retort that it is discomforting and a source of profound dismay to recall that the viewpoint represented by Foucault, that reality is determined by "knowledge," things constructed by words, first became influential in this country in the late sixties and early seventies—about the time the Supreme Court began to issue decisions only tenuously related to the Constitution and other legal documents purportedly under interpretation.[9] Most disturbing in such passages is the diabolical arrogance: while "man" is a mere ideological construct or "configuration," an implicit "we" is possessed of "our knowledge," from which "the naïve"—Chesterton's common men—are excluded.

By 1985, when Justice Brennan made overt his "claim to judicial power to revise the Constitution," in Raoul Berger's pungent phrase, the close association between the new modes of legal and literary interpretation had been recognized and exploited in the work of at least two prominent scholars, the literary critic Stanley Fish and the jurist Ronald Dworkin. At the time, Fish enjoyed a joint appointment in the English Department and the Law School of Duke University, while Dworkin, as Professor of Law at New York University and University Professor of Jurisprudence at Oxford, was a dominant figure on the Anglo-American legal scene. From the perspective of traditional norms of interpretation, these two have so much in common that their clash in the pages of *Critical Inquiry*—flagship journal of postmodernism—is an indication that relativistic, ideological interpretation is so firmly established that its practitioners can confidently debate the details without endangering the "project" as a whole.[10] Both Dworkin and Fish accept the proposition that the meaning of a text, be it a pastoral eclogue or a last will and testament, is constructed by the interpreter out of the words of the text rather than discovered in them. On this decisive point, they are at one not only with each other but with every variety of postmodernism—deconstruction, feminism, New Historicism, cultural materialism, Lacanian psychoanalysis—the whole endless list. Perhaps Justice Brennan's forthright avowal of his "imaginative" method of construing the Constitution was prompted by a sense of the growing body of theoretical support, from a variety of academic disciplines, for what had long been his own practice and that of many of his colleagues. Dworkin is an enemy of what he calls "legal positivism" and regards the kind of liberal judicial activism that he favors as superior on moral grounds. Thus his rhetoric provides support for the vague public-relations sophistries of liberal media commentators and the Supreme Court justices themselves. Fish's arguments, if more cynical, are also more forthright and furnish a far more realistic version of the "politics of interpretation." If the new interpretive paradigm is accepted, then interpretation and politics are virtually interchangeable, and there is no escape from either, and hence no privileged moral status for Dworkin's liberalism. His dilemma is how to confer absolute freedom upon his own interpretive fancies without sliding into the totalitarian abyss represented by the Marxism of Frank Lentricchia, who maintains that only the "pieties of humanist tradition" conceal "a will to power, a constant acitivity of appropriation" in every text and every interpretation.[11]

The career of Stanley Fish as a literary theorist is a paradigm case of this liberal dilemma. He was initially in the vanguard of the reader-response school of criticism, insisting that no text has an intrinsic meaning, a meaning in itself; rather, meaning *is* the experience of the reader. Since it puts extravagant value on the subjective response of the individual, this affective theory could be called the American Civil Liberties Union approach to literature. Just as excessive pre-occupation with civil liberties, to the neglect of civil order, leads to anarchy in society; so reader-response criticism, in its preoccupation with the mental and emotional goings-on in the individual, leads to the disintegration of objective standards and permanent values in literature. Now the reader-response theory had been thoroughly demolished by William K. Wimsatt, Jr., and Monroe C. Beardsley in "The Affective Fallacy," published more than two decades before Fish took the notion up. A critical fixation with reader's response, Wimsatt and Beardsley had argued, "ends in impressionism and skepticism" and "the poem itself, as an object of specifically critical judgment, tends to disappear."[12] Fish acknowledges the force of these strictures without making any effort to demonstrate their inconse-quence. Citing the same passage as I, he remarks, "I shall return to these arguments, not so much to refute them as to affirm and em-brace them."[13] A reading experience of one's own, untrammeled by an independently existing text, becomes, as it were, a literary "civil right." This is a critical stance that reflects political liberalism in a phase of youthful exuberance.

Over against that impetus in liberalism, which demands for everyone the right "to do his own thing," is set that colder, greyer proclivity for collectivism. This polarity is reflected in Fish's gradual abandonment of a commitment to the individual reader's unbridled freedom to interpret as the spirit moves him in favor of what he calls "the authority of interpretive communities." Undoubtedly the most compelling motive for Fish's shifting viewpoint is the simple absurdity of straightforward reader-response criticism, which could satisfy an intelligence as shrewd as his for only so long. But an additional motive may be at work: if meaning lies purely in the response of the reader, *any* reader, then there is no objective criterion for distinguishing between the interpretation of a freshman and a full professor, and the authority and importance of the critic are, at the least, mightily diminished. While reader-response criticism is, thus, a potent weapon for assaulting the fortress of academic prestige, it must be deprecated when one is safely ensconced within the citadel. To be sure, with the new formulation there is still no question of an inherent meaning, or even a complex of meanings, subsisting in a text as such. The generation of meaning is ascribed, however, not to the individual reader, but rather to the institutional norms and expectations of the interpretive community in which the individual is sited. The erstwhile liberated reader is now the prisoner—indeed the creature—of the social situation of which he is inevitably a part. What counts as meaning, as literature, even as argument, is a function of the circumstances of a particular culture with its "interested specifications."[14]

Fish has since settled on what must be called an anti-theory of interpretation on his own account of the matter. In the essay "Consequences" he maintains that no theory *about* interpretation can possibly have consequences for the practice *of* interpretation because the theory itself is an interpretation. There can be no standard by which to measure or judge interpretive practice because all allegedly universal standards or general theories are generated by the exigencies of particular practices they are supposed to guide or explain. Or as Fish puts it:

The argument *against* theory is simply that this substitution of the general for the local has never been and will never be achieved. Theory is an impossible project which will never succeed. It will never succeed simply because the primary data and formal laws necessary to its success will always be spied or picked out from within the contextual circumstances of which they are supposedly independent. The objective facts and rules of calculation that are to ground interpretation and render it principled are themselves interpretive products: they are, therefore, always and already contaminated by the interested judgments they claim to transcend.[15]

Fish asserts that we cannot enter the world of discourse without beliefs: "a belief is a prerequisite for being conscious at all."[16] Theory fails because it seeks to give an independent explanation to beliefs, and "we can never get to the side of our beliefs and, therefore, any perspective we have on one or more of them will be grounded in others of them in relation to which we can have no perspective because we have no distance."[17] This is perhaps no more than to say that we must believe our beliefs or they would not be our beliefs.

Of course from Fish's perspective it is an error to talk about *our* beliefs: they are less ours than we are theirs. This "antifoundationalist" negation of theory, Fish insists, is by no means "an argument for unbridled subjectivity, for the absence of constraints on the individual...in fact, it is an argument for the situated subject, for the individual who is always constrained by the local or community standards and criteria of which his judgment is an extension." The individual can only function within the rules or structures of communal discourse: "That agent cannot distance himself from these rules, because it is only within them that he can think about alternative courses of action or, indeed, think at all."[18] Fish thus dismisses with an insouciant flourish of paradox the charge of relativism that taints his earlier affective theory:

> ...the positing of context- or institution-specific norms surely rules out the possibility of a norm whose validity would be recognized by everyone, no matter what his situation. But it is beside the point for any particular individual, for since everyone is situated somewhere, there is no one for whom the absence of an asituational norm would be of any practical consequence, in the sense that his performance or his confidence in his ability to perform would be impaired. So that while it is generally true that to have many standards is to have none at all, it is not true for anyone in particular (for there is no one in a position to speak "generally"), and therefore it is a truth of which one can say "it doesn't matter."[19]

Now obviously this principle has virtually limitless sociopolitical application beyond the sphere of literature (indeed, the circumference of that sphere, like all others, is itself subject to interpretation). The Constitution, for example, can *only* mean what the judges (or the politicians or the journalists) say it means because any attribution of meaning is someone's interpretation. Strict constructionism would, then, be just one more interpretation, not only of the Constitution but of the rules for reading a document. The controversy over judicial review, Fish says, "is quite literally a demand for theory, for a justifying argument that does not presuppose the interests of any party or the supremacy of any goal or borrow its terms from the practice it would regulate."[20] But like any other text, the Constitution is accessible only through interpretation: "Strictly speaking, getting 'back-to-the-text' is not a move one can perform, because the text one gets back to will be the text demanded by some other interpretaton and that interpretation will be presiding over its production."[21]

Fish's argument has a strong *prima facie* plausibility, which is traceable to two sources, one roughly empirical and the other, ironically, theoretical. First, it is undeniably true that current academic literary criticism presents a bewildering array of conflicting explanations and valuations of the nature and purpose both of literature in general and of specific literary works. (The same kind of confusion is equally evident in most other academic disciplines in the humanities as well as in jurisprudence.) But the present state of affairs in the academic world is by no means normal: the attempt for nearly half a century now to mass-produce college graduates has resulted in an overall hypertrophy of what is called "higher education," with a predictable decline of standards among students and faculty alike. There has been a concomitant proliferation of scholarly publication with a similar decline in the care with which new theories and new readings have been propounded. Hence a great deal of the disagreement about interpretations of literary works is attributable to nothing more than the thirst for novelty among the bored and restless crowds milling about within the ivy-covered walls and the cacophony attendant upon mobs. In addition, what might be called the ideological imperative must be factored in: every text must be subjected to Marxist and feminist reinterpretation; every favored ethnic group or political faction must be granted its cultural "role models" with a place in the "canon." Finally, there is the vocational bias that increasingly intrudes into what is supposed to be liberal education and insists that all meaning is reducible to cost-benefit analysis. It is really no wonder that there is no agreement about truth in the contemporary university, since so few of its denizens are interested in seeking it.

But despite his proclaimed aversion to theory, the second and more potent argument lending credence to Fish's "anti-foundationalist" case rests on the same theoretical foundation as all the other varieties of postmodernism—the arbitrariness of the signifier in the Saussurian theory of language; and it requires the same linguistic sleight of hand as Derridean deconstruction.[22] Words, Fish insists, do not have ascertainable meanings apart from specific contexts. An incident illustrating this proposition furnishes the title of his volume, *Is There a Text in This Class?*. On the first day of the semester, one his colleagues was asked by a student: "Is there a text in this class?" "Yes," the colleague replied, "*The Norton Anthology of English Literature*." "No," the student persisted, "I mean in this class do we believe in poems and things, or is it just us?" Whereupon his colleague thought, "One of Fish's victims!"[23] Not for a moment chagrined, the resourceful Fish sees in this incident his vindication: just as the meaning of the word "text" is contingent upon the particular institutional situation and the occasion on which it is uttered, even so *a* text—*any* text—can only mean to us what the expectations generated by our present conditions allow. The anecdote about confusion over the meaning of "text" shows, further, how new semantic variables can be introduced into a situation.

The effect of Fish's assault upon theory is to make no theory the ultimate theory: to make an absolute out of the relative. Chesterton remarks on the surprise of many observers that St. Thomas Aquinas "does not deal at all with what many now think the main metaphysical question; whether we can prove that the primary act of recognition of any reality is real." The reason for this epistemological reticence, Chesterton claims, is the Saint's realization that without an acceptance of the fundamental data of experience as self-evident, no thought at all, much less philosophy, is possible: "I suppose it is true in a sense that a man can be a fundamental skeptic, but he cannot be anything else; certainly not even a defender of fundamental skepticism."[24] Now what Fish calls "antifoundationalism" is precisely what Chesterton calls "fundamental skepticism." In denying the need, nay, the possibility of providing a theoretical justification for *any* position, Fish effectively declines to be a "defender of fundamental skepticism"—he is rather an exploiter of skepticism. He thus relegates men and women to the status of prisoners in an infinite regress of interpretations—arbitrary and mutable, but ineluctably imposed by the reigning culture. We are thus reduced to witting or unwitting players in a furious political game with ruthlessly enforced but uncertain rules, which are constantly subject to change without notice. Fish's antifoundationalism thus endeavors to make a covert principle of order out of disorder itself.

We may begin by taking solace in the fact that Fish's argument for the absolute instability of texts hangs by the thread of equivocation, a linguistic confusion lurking in certain key terms, particularly "meaning" and "interpretation." With reference to literature, "meaning" comprises at least three distinct (though not wholly separate) *meanings*. First there is the simplest level—what is being described or narrated or generally represented in a work of literature. Interpretation at this level is roughly equivalent to what is offered by a United Nations translator of a diplomat's address. What critics are more likely to disagree about is analogous to the "interpretation" of a speech by network commentators and newspaper editorialists. The basic literal meaning is something that most intelligent, educated readers can agree about with regard to most works of literature. Of course there are works in which even a determination of "what is going on" in the most fundamental sense can be problematic—James Joyce's *Finnegan's Wake* comes to mind. But there is no disagreement among John Dryden, Dr. Johnson, and Stanley Fish about what action is represented in, say, *Paradise Lost*. What the three might well disagree about is the significance, the meaningfulness, or the import of the work, even as commentators and columnists disagree about what a President's speech *means* for the economy, education policy, or the deployment of armed forces. Finally, critics disagree about the *value* of a work of literature, its "meaning" for culture or education; but such disagreement is less likely to involve works that have become established as "great" or "major" or even "important." It might take several centuries for the process to be completed, as in the case of Donne, Herbert, and Marvell, or several generations as with Melville and Dickinson; but once a writer has made it into the list (or "canon"), he stays. The notorious campaign against Milton by T. S. Eliot and F. R. Leavis in the thirties can hardly be said to have disturbed the seventeenth-century poet's place in the school syllabus. Eliot and Leavis themselves never doubted for a moment that Milton was a great poet; they merely sought to diminish his influence and rearrange the rankings.

In arguing that the meaning of texts is created by interpretive communities, wielding cultural norms and discursive rules, Fish overlooks the contrary and more significant fact that interpretive communities are themselves created in part by works of literature, since literature is a constituent of culture. The very texts subject to interpretation are one of the constraints upon any interpreter. Hence Virgil can more properly be said to have generated the conditions of interpretation in Western civilization than the latest scions of that tradition can be said to have created that tradition through interpretation. This state of affairs is even more evident with a document like the Constitution: its authority must be prior to the community that interprets it, because the Constitution—as the term proclaims—*constitutes* that community. In very concrete terms it is the Constitution that establishes the very existence, not to say the authority, of the Supreme Court. Justice Brennan's depreciatory attitude toward the actual words of the document and the intentions of its framers is only one manifestation of a widespread contemporary rebellion of interpreters against the authority and integrity of original documents. In addition to jurists one might well consider many contemporary biblical exegetes and theologians, and of course literary critics. The motivations are brashly laid out by Stanley Fish: if the "practice of literary criticism...is absolutely essential not only to the maintenance of, but to the very production of, the objects of its attention," then "the greatest gain that falls to us...is a greatly enhanced sense of the importance of our activities."[25]

For Fish, the motive of interpretation is interpretation itself, conceived as a mode of appropriation and self-aggrandizement deployed by the self in tension with its community of discourse. For a Marxist like Frank Lentricchia the appropriation is carried out in the name of that hypostatized version of the collective self, revolution. The task of the Marxist academic is, therefore, to appropriate the traditional text for the goals of revolutionary change, to bring out "its politically activist, materially textured substance (made well-nigh invisible by humanist academics)."[26] Neither the liberal nor the Marxist account of interpretation explains why we prefer *Paradise Lost* to Edward Benlowes' *Theophila*, much less why we *should* prefer Milton's poem. Fish's argument for the liberal "persuasive model" of interpretation provides no account of any preferences at all, except perhaps sheer appetite. Every opinion is, finally, of equal validity (or invalidity): "I may, in some sense, *know* that my present reading of *Paradise Lost* follows from assumptions that I did not always hold and may not hold in a year or so, but that 'knowledge' does not prevent me from knowing that my present reading of *Paradise Lost* is the correct one."[27] Only a man completely caught up in the euphoria of professional prestige and affluence could be so utterly oblivious to the recurrent spiritual crisis of modern times—the sense of alienation growing out of the loss of meaning and purpose in life. It is, after all, a principal purpose of a liberal education to provide students with breadth of learning and the critical habits of mind for reflection upon the significance of their existence. Scholars who have abandoned meaning and truth have effectively renounced the heart of their educational mission. Fish's view of interpretation—to fabricate meaning out of the inherently meaningless—seems a last desperate recourse. Passing odd, therefore, is his claim to give the only "coherent account of *dis*agreement." Without some account of human nature prior to its various manifestations in specific cultural settings, Fish cannot explain the very existence of interpretive communities, and he offers no explanation of how any disagreement could ever arise once interpretive communities are in place. How could a creature of such a constraining "community" ever change his mind or disagree about anything? For Fish, however, the only alternative to his persuasion model is apparently unthinkable: "To someone who believes in determinate meaning, disagreement can only be a theological error." There is more than a hint of a sneer when Fish suggests that, apart from his own, "original sin would seem to be the only relevant model" for interpretive "waywardness."[28]

It is probably true that all disagreements are ultimately theological, but traditional modes of interpretation have generally been able to handle disputes without reaching that ultimate point. It is also true that there is something very like original sin involved in most disagreements. Critics argue over interpretations because there is a power or vision in truly talented writers that cannot be denied. Great literature—like the Constitution—is constitutive, and interpretation can be a means of recruiting the powerful vision of the artist to one's own conception of the world. While editorialists judge the value of a politician's speech by the criteria of their own political views, critics interpret the significance—the meaningfulness—of literature in accord with their own *Weltanschauungen*. Apart from the breadth of his knowledge and his sensitivity to technique and style, a critic's perspicacity about literature is to a great extent contingent upon his understanding of life. A critic who bears this in mind and exercises humility will recognize that the truth about life and literature alike will always escape his formulations, which are at best partial; but he will not doubt the existence of truth or give up seeking it. A jurist who resolves to be thus disinterested and fair-minded towards the Constitution, even knowing that the feebleness of his insight and the strength of his personal predilections will prevent him from ever recovering the whole of its meaning (the "original sin" factor), cannot reasonably be accused by Justice Brennan of "false humility." After all, Stanley Fish asssures us that it is the critic who declines to be "the humble servant of texts" (and let us not forget that *non serviam* was *the* original sin) who gains "a greatly enhanced sense of the importance of [his] activities." In devising the "authority of interpretive communities"—which in practice means the dominance of important professors in major universities—Fish assimilates the literary scholar to the mandarin domain of the New Class intellectual. The critic who fancies that he determines, rather than discovers, the truth about literature identifies himself with the technocrats, experts, and professionals who manipulate the values of society in accordance with their own interests and velleities. Life is a game in which all the rules are subject to qualification and exception, and success goes to the man clever enough to keep up with the constantly shifting landscape or assertive enough to impose his own will on it. The most widely known and publicly consequential manifestation of this mentality, as expounded by Justice Brennan, comes from the realm of jurisprudence: for more than a quarter of a century abortion has been a "Constitutional right" in America (along with almost the whole of the industrialized West) because it serves the aims and appeals to the whims of the deracinated intellectual and professional classes who thrive in a bureaucratic welfare state. Similarly, Milton, Faulkner, Jane Austen—name your writer—are to be interpreted and taught by a hermeneutic that represents the prejudices of those same classes.[29] The factor linking *Roe v. Wade* and contemporary literary theory is that the actual words of a text, as well as the truth represented by the text, are simply irrelevant in the face of political zealotry.

This calculated neglect of the truth renders problematic the integrity and purpose of both courts of law and universities. The concept of academic freedom, long regarded as the very air that university scholars breathe, becomes especially equivocal, and Stanley Fish's notion of the interpretive community highlights the contradictions. An interpretive community, he says, is "not so much a group of individuals who shared a point of view, but a point of view or way of organizing experience that shared individuals in the sense that its assumed distinctions, categories of understanding, and stipulations of relevance and irrelevance were the content and consciousness of community members who were therefore no longer individuals, but, insofar as they were embedded in the community's enterprise, community property."[30] This assertion is, of course, another rejoinder to the accusation of relativism leveled against the schema of the interpretive community. Fish follows here the paradigm of Jean Jacques Rousseau: an initial assertion of virtually limitless freedom (reader-response criticism) turns into total constraint, with the individual reader or interpreter figured as a blind prisoner of the collective mind. Fish has come to recognize, however, that his effort to resolve the problem of relativism produces another complaint that he must confront: "the privileging of the interpretive community leaves us without an adequate account of change."[31] He circumvents this obstacle by maintaining "that an interpretive community...is an engine of change":

> It is an engine of change because its assumptions are not a
> mechanism for shutting out the world but for organizing it,
> for seeing phenomena as already related to the interests and
> goals that make the community what it is. The community,
> in other words, is always engaged in doing work, the work
> of transforming the landscape into material for its project;
> but that project is then itself transformed by the very work
> it does.[32]

For Stanley Fish this is an uncharacteristically thoughtless argument: it may be called an "account of change," but only of change
that cannot make a difference because there is nothing permanent
against which to measure it. It may be an explanation of interpretation, but only of meaningless interpretation. The interpretive
community, like the individual interpreter, turns out to be the
blind prisoner of the circumstances that constitute it: it is an "engine
of change" with no driver and no direction. This is a state of affairs
attractive to a sophist, but, as Chesterton points out, it is not reality
but an illusion of sophistry: "Most thinkers, on realising the
apparent mutability of being, have really forgotten their own
realisation of the being, and believed only in the mutability. They
cannot even say that a thing changes into another thing; for them
there is no instant in the process at which it is a thing at all. It is only
a change."[33]

   More striking than Fish's banal argument is his example, which
has sinister implications for the ideal of academic freedom—a principle instituted for protection of the scholar in the pursuit of truth.
A student in Fish's graduate seminar in literary theory comes to him
and admits that in the course of the semester he has changed his
mind about the nature of literary meaning: he now believes it to be

a matter of interpretive convention rather than an inherent property of the text. "What bothered him," Fish writes, "was the very fact that he had been persuaded, for, given those same views, he didn't see how his mind could ever have been changed."[34] The troubled young man cannot understand, that is, what has impelled him from one interpretive community (old-fashioned "formalists") into another (postmodern pragmatists—little Fishes). Since the student is himself a graduate assistant, teaching an introductory literature course, Fish merely points out to him that the same arguments propounded by his graduate professor would have been considerably less persuasive coming from a student in his own class. To be sure, Fish attempts to soften the dictatorial implications of this example:

> I am not suggesting that the mere fact of my position as instructor was sufficient to make my assertions the stimulus to change; it is easy to imagine an instructor who did not command respect because he had not thought through the implications of his argument or, from the other side, a student whose performance had been so impressive that an instructor would feel obliged to come to terms with anything she said. But in any of these circumstances it would still be the case that change, in the form of the reconsideration of received opinion, would be prompted by a suggestion that came from a source assumed in advance to be, if not authoritative, at least weighty.[35]

For my part, it is difficult to imagine what could constitute a well-conceived, persuasive argument or an "impressive performance" able to disrupt the complacency of the interpretive community, since the criteria for clarity, persuasiveness, and impressiveness are always predetermined by one or another interpretive community and, according to Fish's account, *have no other source.* What he calls "easy to imagine" is in fact impossible even to conceive in a situation without objective norms existing independently of the situation itself. What is all too "easy to imagine" is a professor who knows exactly how he expects his students to answer, or a student—even a rather dull student—who instinctively senses just how intolerant his professor is, just where the professsor stands in the departmental pecking order, and just how "weighty" his professional reputation currently is.

Fish closes his essay "Change" with a statement epitomizing the prevalent conception of liberal education and its corollary, academic freedom. Liberal education has nothing to do with the liberality of spirit that enables one to value truth, and academic freedom does not provide the freedom to seek the truth that truly sets one free. Rather, the entire enterprise is geared toward the professoriat's preoccupation with self-interest:

> Perhaps the most persistent charge against the notion of interpretive communities is that it seems to make disciplinary and professional activity its own end. But since that end itself is continually changing, the charge can be cheerfully embraced because it says only that members of a community will always believe in the ends for which they work, and that therefore their work will never be ended even though it will be ceaselessly transformed.[36]

It is doubtless ill-bred to wonder, at least out loud, how "cheerfully" taxpayers, alumni, and donors can be expected to embrace the prospect of supporting a costly activity whose only purpose is to alleviate the restlessness and reinforce the egos of its agents; that is, to help bored, discontented academics find something new to say and thereby feel "if not authoritative, at least weighty." Of course both the weight and the authority are rather illusory, since they have no source in the interpretive community, as Fish conceives it, other than an individual's personal magnetism, which is always fragile, or the interests of the institution itself, which must necessarily be "ceaselessly transformed," having no more stable foundation than the shifting sands of circumstance. As we know from the Gospel, sand is a notoriously shaky foundation—or "anti-foundation"—on which to build a house (Matthew 7.26). In this scheme academic freedom permits the change of anything and everything all the time, but it does not permit permanence. The one forbidden claim is the claim to truth, which is the fundamental need of a free, rational creature. The enslaved "members" of such a totalitarian "community" will always "believe in the ends for which they work" with the same conviction that ducks will always quack.

Fish's model of interpretation is reprehensible, but it has the virtue of forthrightness. Unlike most proponents of postmodernism, he pushes his critical observations and intuitions to their logical conclusion with the bracing result of evaporating illusions. If we abandon the belief that texts embody intrinsic meaning and become "antifoundationalists," we are not thereby released into a world of unconstrained interpretive freedom: we still must "act in accordance with standards and norms that are the content of our beliefs and, therefore, the very structure of our consciousness." There is no "moment of unconstrained choice," no mental locus outside our own personal history and the history of our culture as it impinges on us, that would enable an objective, theoretical judgment of those beliefs: "an antifoundationalist (like anyone else) can always reject something because its source has been shown to be some piece of human history he finds reprehensible, but an antifoundationalist cannot (without at that moment becoming a foundationalist) reject something simply because its source has been shown to be human history as opposed to something independent of it."[37] "Human history" here cloaks the familiar postmodernist appeal to *materialist historicism*. If there is no standard, no meaning, independent of a human consciousness produced by the material circumstances of "history," then any rejection of a "something" found "reprehensible" can only be arbitrary or whimsical, since the something and the disapproval are alike inevitable products of the same "human history." Morality cannot guide interpretation, for it, too, is just more interpretation. If this state of affairs obtains, the self-righteous indignation so typical of postmodernist academics has all the dignity of a spoilt child's temper tantrum.

It is the very blatancy of his view that makes Fish a superb critic of more evasive liberals like Ronald Dworkin. Just as Fish looks at legal interpretation from the perspective of a literary critic, so Dworkin tries to enlist literary interpretation as a means of reinforcing his opinions on jurisprudence. His aim is to show that "legal practice is an exercise in interpretation not only when lawyers interpret particular documents or statutes but generally. Law so conceived is deeply and thoroughly political. Lawyers and judges cannot avoid politics in the broad sense of political theory."[38] So far this sounds like Fish, but what follows is just fishy. Dworkin wants to maintain that meaning cannot be simply discovered "there" in the legal text, that it is generated by interpretation, but also that the interpreter is not simply free to "make up" the law, or impose his will under the guise of interpretation; moreover—and this is the crucial issue—he wants to maintain that some interpretations are *better* because of some political principle. It is to establish this point that Dworkin brings in his "aesthetic hypothesis" as an analogy from literary criticism:

> Interpretation of a text attempts to show *it* as the best work
> of art *it* can be, and the pronoun insists on the difference

between explaining a work of art and changing it into a different one. Perhaps Shakespeare could have written a better play based on the sources he used for *Hamlet* than he did, and in that better play the hero would have been a more forceful man of action. It does not follow that *Hamlet*, the play he wrote, really is like that after all. Of course a theory of interpretation must contain a subtheory about identity of a work of art in order to be able to tell the difference between interpreting and changing a work. (Any useful theory of identity will be controversial, so that this is one obvious way in which disagreements in interpretation will depend on more general disagreements in aesthetic theory.)[39]

Just as literary interpretation must enhance the aesthetic value of the work, "so an interpretation of any body or division of law...must show the value of that body of law in political terms by demonstrating the best principle or policy it can be taken to serve."[40]

As Stanley Fish observes, Dworkin does not really grasp the implications of the model of interpretation that he tries to assume; he "repeatedly falls away from his own best insight into a version of the two fallacies (of pure subjectivity and pure objectivity) he so forcefully challenges."[41] Fish's point is that, on the antifoundationalist model, there can be no tension between text and interpreter because both are creations of the interpretive community. We can add that if meaning does not, in some sense, subsist "there" in the text of *Hamlet*, then no interpretation can be objectively *wrong* (though it can be more or less persuasive to various individuals). If meaning is only available through interpretation, then a "wrong" interpretation could only be "corrected" by another interpretation since there is no independent objective standard. "A subtheory about identity of a work of art" can in no way judge the faithfulness of an interpretation to a *Hamlet* that can only exist in someone's interpretation, because the "subtheory" is itself just another interpretation. A practical demonstration of the problem comes when Dworkin posits, as an example of an impossible literary interpretation, a reading of Agatha Christie mysteries that treats them as serious philosophical novels rather than mere detective fiction. Fish gleefully cites a half dozen academic studies published since 1979 that do just that and, for good measure, throws in his own rudimentary sketch of Christie's "theory of evil."[42] If there is no "foundation" for thought in reality, then men and women will think whatever comes into their heads, and there will be no distinguishing among thoughts that arise from genetic quirks, from peer-group pressure, or from toxic chemicals in the environment.

Dworkin's attempted rejoinder is opaque and finally banal. In order to preserve an "independent objective reality" while still demanding the interpretive freedom to manipulate reality in accord with the liberal agenda, he effectively shatters that reality, or at least our modes of knowing it, into disconnected fragments:

Someone might say that my position is the deepest possible form of skepticism about morality, art, and interpretation because I am actually saying that moral or aesthetic or interpretive judgments cannot possibly describe an independent objective reality. But that is not what I said. I said that the question of what "independence" and "reality" are, for any practice, is a question within that practice, so that whether moral judgments can be objective is itself a moral question, and whether there is objectivity in interpretation is itself a question of interpretation. This threatens to make skepticism not inevitable but impossible.[43]

A little skepticism would be a merciful relief from such willful credulity. In the thirteenth century, Averroist philosophers asserted that individual men share one common intellect and hence lack their own immortal souls. In order to square this position with Christianity, some members of the school seem to have flirted with the theory that propositions could be true from the standpoint of philosophical reason while false in terms of the faith required by revelation.[44] St. Thomas Aquinas quotes an unnamed opponent as follows: "Through reason I conclude that the intellect is necessarily one in number; however, I firmly hold the opposite through faith."[45] For this doctrine of "two truths," Dworkin offers a potential infinity of "truths," depending on which professional discipline or personal predilection might be engaging one's attention.

Ronald Dworkin provides a classic case of wanting to have it both ways. In an essay arguing for his own version of liberalism, he rejects the conservative view of equality, which "means treating him [each person] the way the good or truly wise person would wish to be treated," in favor of a "theory of equality [which] supposes that political decisions must be, so far as possible, independent of any particular conception of the good life, or of what gives value to life."[46] If not merely disingenuous, this view is patently absurd as it stands, since a government that affects neutrality towards the values and practices of its citizens is obviously influencing and deciding about morality, insofar as it implies that traditional moral virtues are not especially important. Dworkin makes the inconsistency of this putative moral neutrality explicit in a subsequent essay in which he recommends his own conception of "liberalism based on equality": "It rests on a positive commitment to an egalitarian morality and provides, in that morality, a firm contrast to the economics of privilege."[47] Issues like sodomy, adultery, and divorce are matters of "private morality"—outside the pale of governmental concern, despite the enormous consequences of sexual conduct for individuals and society as a whole. Economic egalitariansim, however, is to be enforced by the various agencies of the government with self-righteous moral fervor. For Dworkin the courts, especially, are merely an instrument for enacting his curiously selective notion of "egalitarian morality" into law; "interpretation" is a way of making the Constitution say what liberalism says. Roe v. Wade is the consummate example: as Eva Rubin (a supporter of the decision) has shown, Roe was the culmination of a "litigation campaign," which, like an election campaign, is "essentially pressure-group activity tailored to fit the format of a lawsuit but specifically designed to produce social change rather than to vindicate the private rights of the parties."[48] On this account, Roe v. Wade is plainly an instance of the political corruption of the Supreme Court and of judicial procedures: the only criterion of such "interpretation" is the will to power of the interpreter.

This consideration of current interpretive theories provides a perspective not only on the Constitutional crisis that has emerged in the United States at the close of the twentieth century,[49] but also on the legalism and litigiousness of contemporary society. The manipulative mode of reading the Constitution proposed by Justice William Brennan is not a personal peculiarity of his, and it is not confined to a few jurists or even to the practice of jurisprudence; rather it is a predictable outgrowth of broad trends in postmodern scholarship in a variety of disciplines. In the hands of judges like Brennan and theoreticians like Dworkin, laws are detached from any conception of the Law, human or divine, that stands independent of positively enacted legislation, giving it genuine authority and legitimacy. Nowadays public complaints about criminals who "get off" because sharp lawyers exploit "legal technicalities" are quite frequent; but if there is no fundamental or intrinsic distinction between right and wrong, then laws can be nothing but technicalities. That is, they are "techniques," modes of verbal power by which those who know how to appropriate them impose their will; or, as Thrasymachus puts it in the first book of the *Republic*, "the just is nothing but the advantage of the stronger."[50] When the anti-foundational basis of the judicial views of a Brennan or a Dworkin are laid out by an unblushing postmodernist like Stanley Fish, it becomes clear what is logically entailed is an abandonment of any objective conception of justice based on the reality of human nature. When the liberal arts are corrupted by postmodern literary theory, the public—which has absorbed the vicious precepts of a multitude of contemporary sophists, each a Thrasymachus in modern dress—becomes unable to affirm the inherent reality of justice and truth. Thus a decline in higher education portends a general moral and spiritual malaise in the culture of a nation.

CHAPTER SIX

Distinct Models: Why We Teach What We Teach

In his commendatory poem in the first folio edition of Shakespeare's *Comedies, Histories, and Tragedies* (1623), Ben Jonson addresses the Bard as "Soul of the age!" (17); however, a couple of dozen lines later, Jonson proclaims, "He was not of an age, but for all time" (43).[1] The apparent contradiction between these lines provides an excellent teaching device, because it forces students to confront the complexity of artistic greatness: an author like Shakespeare is great because he expresses vividly and concretely a particular time, place, and culture; and yet he transcends what is merely local and ephemeral and touches the perennial and universal concerns of humanity by means of what is immediate and particular. That students should find this paradox difficult to grasp is not surprising, but it is troubling to witness eminent scholars of literature and the other humane disciplines quite as nonplussed by Jonson's paradoxical tribute as the most callow sophomore. According to the reigning heterodoxy, absolutely nothing is "for all time"; and works of literature do not bespeak the "soul of the age," so much as they conceal, even while embodying, its ideological and economic imperatives. Hence the current clamor from powerful forces within the academy of the "opening up" or dismantling of the "canon" of "classic" works, for the abolition of the very notion of "great books." Should this view prevail, then the question, "Why we teach what we teach?", would be no longer moot, but merely meaningless. Although *pretexts* for teaching this or that *text* would abound, there could be no *reasons*, since rational discrimination among the "products" of deterministic cultural hegemonies is impossible. If a work of art, literature, or philosophy is not intrinsically valuable, is not great on its own merits, then it can only be of interest as an event or phenomenon, exercising more or less influence over the course of history. It is, therefore, important to attempt an understanding of how Shakespeare—or Plato, or Dante, or Jefferson, or Jane Austen—can be both "Soul of the age" and "for all time." Although the following discussion will deal principally with poetry, this is largely a matter of convenience, because the poems are sufficiently succinct to be compared briefly. As Cicero points out, "All the arts, which pertain to humanity, have a certain common bond and are joined together among themselves as it were by a certain kinship."[2] It is this element of common humanity that is crucial to curricular decisions and is, indeed, the only basis for the integrity of university professors as scholars and teachers.

Perhaps the only conceivable benefit of the current assault on Western culture from among the ranks of its putative conservators is that we are forced to reflect upon what it is and why it is worth conserving. First, it is important to recognize that what is at stake is no mere urge to modify or expand the canon, or list of great works, no sincere argument over the criteria for the admission of authors and titles to the curriculum, much less over the inclusion or exclusion of this or that particular work. The issue is whether a hierarchy of works can be established at all, whether rational (and hence just) norms for determining intellectual, moral, and aesthetic excellence are possible. A negative answer to this question involves not "opening up" the curriculum, but eviscerating it; and if there is no defensible tradition of great works—no "canon"—then it is difficult to justify the study of literature, art, philosophy, and humane letters from any perspective other than social science. Professors of the humanities will seem less like scholars in academic disciplines than vultures and jackals feeding on the cadaver of the liberal arts. Hence Barbara Herrnstein Smith was somewhat disingenuous when she used the occasion of her 1988 MLA Presidential Address to sneer at "members of the association who still regard women as members of another species and are still waiting for the theory fad to blow over," and to insinuate that distress about the present state of affairs in the academic world arose from "the comparison of Oedipus with Sherlock Holmes or the assignment of *The Color Purple* alongside *The Scarlet Letter*."[3]

The revolutionaries who currently dominate academic discourse in the humanities are not really interested in gaining acceptance for *The Color Purple* as a great book, or in gaining a new critical purchase on *The Scarlet Letter*. Revision of the literary canon—both by addition and revaluation—has been old news for a long time. The concept is available, for example, in T. S. Eliot's 1919 essay, "Tradition and the Individual Talent," where he remarks, "The existing monuments form an ideal order among themselves, which is modified by the introduction of the new (really new) work of art among them."[4] Determining the criteria for and the identity of the "really new" work and assessing its precise effect upon and place in the tradition are undertakings subject to reasonable, tolerant, and even fruitful debate. But this is *not* the nature of the disputes of the last three decades, and Barbara Herrnstein Smith could have found this out by stepping down the hall and conferring with some of her Duke colleagues. "Literature is inherently nothing," Frank Lentricchia avers; "or it is inherently a body of rhetorical strategies waiting to be seized."[5] As we have seen,[6] Lentricchia illustrates the practice of ideological expropriation by treating Wallace Stevens' brief poem, "Anecdote of the Jar," written more than three quarters of a century ago, as an attack on American intervention in Viet Nam.

Jane Tompkins, formerly a member of the Duke literature faculty, furnishes an even more efficient model of political hermeneutics in her minute analyses of the "Western" fiction of such writers as Zane Grey and Louis L'Amour (that's "Western" as in "bang-bang, you're dead"; not as in Western civilization). If literature is merely a bundle of "rhetorical strategies" anyway, it would hardly seem to matter which bundle the critic begins with. In fact, the Western offers a distinct advantage: part of the greatness of great literature is precisely the resistance it offers to ideological reductivism and ordinary oversimplification. "Anecdote of the Jar" as anti-war poem is not really a very convincing interpretation, and a penitent Frank Lentricchia, writing a few years later, observes that the postmodern critical enterprise relies on incompetence, whether deliberate or unwitting:

To be certified as an academic literary critic, you need to believe, and be willing to assert, that Ezra Pound's *Cantos*, a work twice the length of *Paradise Lost*, and which 99 percent of all serious students of literature find too difficult to read, actually forwards the cause of worldwide anti-Semitism. You need to tell your students that, despite what almost a century's worth of smart readers have concluded, Joseph Conrad's *Heart of Darkness* is a subtle celebration of the desolations of imperialism. My objection is not that literary study has been politicized, but that it proceeds in happy indifference to, often in unconscionable innocence of, the protocols of literary competence. Only ten to fifteen years ago, the views I've cited on Pound and Conrad would have received barely passing grades had they been submitted as essays in an undergraduate course. Now, such views circulate at the highest levels of my profession in the essays of distinguished literary critics.[7]

One might only demur that it is politicization that inevitably necessitates the incompetence, precisely because genuine works of literary art retain their own meaning and integrity despite the efforts of academic ideologues to turn them into verbose bumper stickers.

Hence the great advantage of "popular culture" as a new object of scholarly attention: much popular literature has insufficient substance of its own to put up a real fight and can be made to say pretty much whatever the critic wishes. Jane Tompkins manhandles *Hondo* and *Riders of the Purple Sage* like a wrangler breaking timid Shetland ponies, which submit with hardly a whimper: "What I want to argue for specifically here is the idea that the Western owes its essential character to the dominance of a women's culture in the nineteenth century and to women's invasion of the public sphere between 1880 and 1920." This essay in the *cherchez la femme* school of literary interpretation concludes triumphantly in this wise: "The Western doesn't have anything to do with the West as such. It isn't about the encounter between civilization and the frontier. It is about men's fear of losing their hegemony and hence their identity, both of which the Western tirelessly reinvents."[8] This bit of ideological demystification is difficult to square with my own experience, since the only regular reader of Westerns of my acquaintance is my own mother, who regarded them as cheap, disposable entertainment. To my knowledge, she has never been afflicted with hegemony envy. Zane Grey and Louis L'Amour, along with their readers, might well have been baffled by the array of semantic doves and rabbits that Tompkins pulls out of their ten-gallon hats; however, seasoned perusers of contemporary academic theory will recognize the sleight-of-hand and the semiological stage properties, as the ideological buckboard rumbles across the textual plain, scattering signifiers like so many tumbleweeds.

What unites Tompkins' approach with all the postmodernists whom we have considered is the *privileging* of the work of the interpreter over the text—the putative object of interpretation. Such an exaltation of the role of the critic has been, as we have seen, the major project of Tompkins' husband Stanley Fish, former chairman of the Duke English Department, through all the transmogrifications of his interpretive enterprise. Abandoning the idea that any piece of writing embodies inherent truth and ascribing its meaning wholly to the activities of the critic will provide "a greatly enhanced sense of the importance of our own activities" and show that "the practice of literary criticism is not something one must apologize for."[9] Under this dispensation, then, neither *The Scarlet Letter* nor *The Scarlet Pimpernel*, neither *The Color Purple* nor *Riders of the Purple Sage* has any intrinsic significance. These "texts" and all others exist solely as a result of the critic's conjuring. Insofar as this interpretive theory is given credence, the canon of great books can scarcely be more than a record of the ideological impositions of regnant "cultural hegemonies." But if such is "the practice of literary criticism," then apologies are certainly in order: in this scheme the critic is no more than an illusionist—a huckster noisily calling attention to his own contrivances. Or the critic is Humpty Dumpty: works, like words, mean exactly what he says they mean. But we all know what happened to Humpty Dumpty, and the fate of literary study in the universities increasingly responsive to market forces and cost-benefit analyses may be similar if critical theory continues to be presented as self-indulgent sophistry.

Such a critical practice is not without its practical pedagogical consequences. As early as a decade ago, members of the English Department at Syracuse University issued a manifesto entitled "Not a Good Idea: A New Curriculum at Syracuse." The authors (eleven in all) exemplify the difficulty of designing a curriculum in a vacuum, literally not knowing what you are talking about:

> The first element that allowed our discussions to maintain collectivity with neither the support of a common canon nor the envelope of an indifferent critical pluralism was the recognition that we had to live, uncomfortably, with our pedagogical object as somehow displaced. Whether in the language of alienation, of repression, of loss, or of self-division, we faced a common awareness that the assumption of a self-evident object of study disappeared along with the closed canon that once incarnated it.[10]

Having "lost" the "object" of their work (which seems uncommonly careless), the professors were forced to fall back on their own predilections; and "the construction of a new curriculum" was expressly an exercise in self-interest: "By 1985 it had become clear that the actual teaching and research interests of the department were no longer adequately served by the curriculum as it stood" (p. 2). The impact upon students of substituting their teachers' hobbies for a genuine curriculum is predictable and made quite explicit by the Syracuse document:

> For those committed to understanding and resisting the role of texts in producing oppressive race, class and gender re-

lations, the end of an education in literature will be, not the traditional "well read" student, but a student capable of critique—of actively pressuring, resisting and questioning cultural texts. The consequences for a curriculum will be a shift from privileging a particular body of culturally sanctioned texts to emphasizing the modes of critical inquiry one can bring to bear on any textual object and the political implications of such modes. (p. 1)

If "textual objects" are "inherently nothing," if their very existence is a result of interpretation, naturally the task of a literature professor is to guide the student in the formation of politically correct attitudes, and liberal education is reduced to training in fashionably sanctimonious carping. That the students might learn more about their professors' prejudices than the substance of their courses has heretofore been regarded as one of the pitfalls of the university; now inculcation in *odium academicum* would seem to be the *sole purpose* of courses utterly devoid of substance in themselves.

In order to see fully the implications of such curricular sansculottism, we must recall that curriculum—what we teach—is ancillary to education; and that *education* ought to be understood in the root sense of the word. The Latin *educare* means to "rear or bring up (children or young animals)," and it in turn derives from *educere*, "to lead forth" or "to lead out of." Implicit in the term is the idea that education consists in leading the young *out* of something, and the something out of which everyone must be led is the peculiar, self-interested ego; for to be self-centered is the common predicament—that narrow, stifling subjectivism that is the universal prison of all human beings. A great work of literature is, then, a book that extends our horizons, that alters our perspective, that makes us take notice of something beyond our immediate needs and desires. Note that the new curriculum proposed in the Syracuse document encourages students to question "cultural texts" and apply a pervasive skepticism to virtually everything except themselves. Similarly, the editors of a new collection of essays on seventeenth-century poetry promote their book as "deeply skeptical of the received ideas about a literature that is itself sensitive to the disruption of epistemological, social, and economic certainties." The essays constitute "a skeptical interrogation," they say, "of numerous received ideas along a variety of fronts."[11] Notice that again what gets questioned or "interrogated" is the literature, or at least the "received ideas" about it (and this amounts to the same thing, since postmodern theory does not allow for the existence of literature apart from interpretation).

A caveat is necessary at this point: valuable as learning is, it is not a substitute for more important virtues. One source of disillusionment with liberal education—especially with a great books curriculum—is that the tradition of Arnoldian humanism has often oversold it as a replacement for religion and conventional moral instruction. As a consequence it has become vulnerable to postmodernist disparagement. Stanley Fish, for example, disdains the reading lists proffered by Robert Alter and Wayne Booth:

> If the truly great works are those that irresistibly invite us to lead a richer and fuller life, why have so many readers of the books Alter and Booth list managed to resist the invitation and gone on from reading Shakespeare and Goethe to acts of incredible cruelty? And why, conversely, have readers of supposedly inferior stuff—works of popular and even "low" culture—been moved by their reading to acts of great altruism and service?[12]

Terry Eagleton is equally scornful of F. R. Leavis's idea that reading great literature "made you a better person": "When the Allied troops moved into the concentration camps some years after the founding of *Scrutiny*, to arrest commandants who had whiled away their leisure hours with a volume of Goethe, it appeared that someone had some explaining to do."[13]

All other things being equal, a sound liberal education is likely to enhance the moral and spiritual sense of a student, but it is not going to inculcate religion and virtue. "Knowledge is one thing," Cardinal Newman writes, "virtue is another; good sense is not conscience, refinement is not humility, nor is largeness and justness of view faith." A liberal education is a worthwhile attainment: a person will generally be better with it than he would have been without it, though it may also add strength and lustre to bad qualities as well as good. An education is certainly not a sufficient provision for moral decency, much less sanctity. Newman's vivid description of the limitations of higher education provides an antidote to the postmodernist accusation that it has failed because it does not automatically produce outstanding virtue:

> Quarry the granite rock with razors, or moor the vessel with a thread of silk; then may you hope with such keen and delicate instruments as human knowledge and human reason to contend against those giants, the passion and the pride of man.[14]

The analogies are exact: the keen razor and the delicate silken thread are among the appurtenances of civilization; they do not confer civilization. Although they are truly instruments for cutting and binding, they are only effective for voluntary tasks in a cultivated environment. A clean-shaven face and needlework with silk presuppose the establishment of a high degree of civility.

The study of great literature must be an integral part of the education of the individual in a civilized society, but it cannot create civilization. There is a grave irony in our efforts to provide a "college education" for everyone even as the general moral and cultural refinement of our communities are disintegrating before our eyes. It is important to conserve the literary heritage of the West, but we may have to face the grim reality that the work of scholarship in the coming century may resemble nothing so much as the work of cloistered scribes during the Dark Ages. Scholars in this new Waste Land will face a technological barbarism, purveying a virtual sandstorm of vulgarity; and their chief task may well be as handmaids to the enhancement of the moral and religious virtues. It will certainly not be a time for literary theorists of any persuasion to revel in self-importance. Nonetheless, although it is a sufficiently humble task, to introduce students to great works of literature is not an ignoble calling.

To be sure, not every piece of literature that is subjected to critical scrutiny in the classroom, much less in the scholar's carrel, is a deathless classic, embodying the perennial wisdom of Western Civilization. Such works should be at the heart of the curriculum, but they are not the whole story. Many poems, plays, and stories are important because they exemplify their own culture so vividly; others exert a powerful influence over subsequent cultural development, and still others unveil so acutely the particularities of individual lives of surpassing interest that they serve to open the eyes of students to a new world. We can tell the difference between a great work of literary art and a mere document—between *Hamlet* and a bill of sale—with absolute certainty, even as we can distinguish midnight from noon. There are, however, crepuscular hours when it is difficult to know when day ends and night begins. The Constitution of the United States, it seems to me, is largely important as an historical and political document: it should be pored over in a course in political philosophy or history, but I do not teach it in my American literature survey. The Declaration of Independence, however, is a powerful

piece of rhetoric to which I usually devote half a class period. Then
there are works that meet every criterion: Plato's *Republic* comes to
mind—it is a crucial influence in the development of Western Civilization; it is an inexhaustible source of moral, political, and metaphysical wisdom; as a pervasively ironic dialogue filled with inge-
nious myths, it is a consummate work of literary art. There are, in
other words, numerous reasons for teaching a wide variety of works
in literature classes. If a teacher concentrates on selecting works for
their excellence of style and thought and their influence and historical importance, then diversity will take care of itself.

Students in my American literature survey, for example, read the
poems of Anne Bradstreet. Although she is by no means a great writer,
her competent, if undistinguished verse provides an invaluable
window into the daily life of colonial Massachusetts, a matrix of
American culture. Moreover, the poems reveal a great deal about the
fortitude and generosity of Bradstreet's own wholly admirable character. "Before the Birth of One of Her Children" is not especially
distinguished either for the elegance of its versification or the inge-
nuity of its figurative language; and its opening lines, in stating the
inevitability of sorrow and death, are commonplace in thought and
sentiment. The conclusion, however, is genuinely moving *because* we
know that the poem is an authentic expression of the situation and
feeling of the author:

> And if I see not half my days that's due,
> What nature would, God grant to yours and you;
> The many faults that well you know I have
> Let be interred in my oblivious grave;
> If any worth or virtue were in me,
> Let that live freshly in thy memory
> And when thou feel'st no grief, as I no harms,

Yet love thy dead, who long lay in thine arms.
And when thy loss shall be repaid with gains
Look to my little babes, my dear remains.
And if thou love thyself, or loved'st me,
These O protect from step-dame's injury.
And if chance to thine eyes shall bring this verse,
With some sad sighs honour my absent hearse;
And kiss this paper for thy love's dear sake,
Who with salt tears this last farewell did take.[15]

This poem furnishes an occasion for pointing out to contemporary students the perils of motherhood in the era before antiseptics and antibiotics, and the prevalence of wicked stepmothers in fairy tales can be ascribed to the simple fact that high maternal mortality in pre-industrial societies resulted in many broken families much as divorce does in our time. A more compelling reason for teaching this poem is the simple dignity with which it expresses both a fearful realization of the possibility of death and courage in the face of that fear, both anxiety over the fate of her motherless children and trust in the love of a husband who can be so candidly addressed. Anne Bradstreet's poems are not intrinsically great literature as, say, Jane Austen's novels are, but they are worth studying because they are the testament of a woman of great fortitude and spiritual depth in a crucial and difficult stage in American history.

If I teach Anne Bradstreet in spite of her mediocrity in strictly literary terms, then Michael Wigglesworth's *The Day of Doom* finds a place because of its ineptitude. I generally ask the class to consider the stanzas where Christ explains to the souls of unbaptized infants why they are justly adjudged to hell, along with hardened sinners, only for having inherited the guilt of Adam's original sin:

Would you have griev'd to have received
    through *Adam* so much good,
As had been your for evermore,
    if he at first had stood?
Would you have said, we ne'r obey'd,
    nor did thy Laws regard;
It ill befits with benefits,
    us, Lord, so to reward?

Since then to share in his welfare,
    you could have been content,
You may with reason share in his treason,
    and in the punishment. (Stanzas 174-75)[16]

Several stanzas further on (the poem runs to more than 200 just like these) the souls of the unbaptized infants trudge ruefully off to hell, though with this small consolation:

A crime it is, therefore in bliss
    you may not hope to dwell;
But unto you I shall allow
    the easiest room in Hell.
The glorious King thus answering,
    they cease, and plead no longer:
Their Consciences must needs confess
    his Reasons are the stronger. (Stanza 181)

There is some value in exposing students to a negative exemplum and to a worldview that is eccentric and unpalatable by modern standards, but it is still more important to show how an awkward style and a logic that is both obtuse and hairsplitting are the marks of a superficial mind failing to come to grips with a profoundly

serious, if terrible, doctrine. *The Day of Doom* was exceedingly
popular in colonial New England, but I suspect that its appeal to
seventeenth-century youth was akin to the effect upon their
modern counterparts of that series of horror films featuring a
dreadfully disfigured villain in desperate need of a manicure: Christ
the Judge as Freddy Krueger.

There are, then, sound pedagogical reasons for teaching the
poetry of Bradstreet and Wigglesworth in undergraduate literature
courses, but the same ends could be attained with, say, the prose of
William Bradford and Thomas Shepard. The exact composition of
a syllabus often depends on what is included in the most conve-
niently available anthologies. But there are some writers who should
be included in every American literature anthology and every syllabus. Consider the following poem, written some two centuries
after *The Day of Doom*, and dedicated to the same theme of our eternal destiny:

> Because I could not stop for Death—
> He kindly stopped for me—
> The Carriage held but just Ourselves—
> And Immortality.
>
> We slowly drove—He knew no haste
> And I had put away
> My labor and my leisure too,
> For His Civility—
>
> We passed the School, where Children strove
> At Recess—in the Ring—
> We passed the Fields of Gazing Grain—
> We passed the Setting Sun—

Or rather—He passed Us—
The Dews drew quivering and chill—
For only Gossamer, my Gown—
My Tippet—only Tulle—

We paused before a House that seemed
A Swelling of the Ground—
The Roof was scarcely visible—
The Cornice—in the Ground—

Since then—'tis Centuries—and yet
Feels shorter than the Day
I first surmised the Horses' Heads
Were toward Eternity—[17]

This, of course, is Emily Dickinson, who turns the common meter
hymn stanza, the same verse form that Michael Wigglesworth
reduces to jog-trot doggerel, into as subtle a vehicle for poetry as
Death's elusive "Carriage." While Bradstreet and Wigglesworth
are important—in different ways—largely because of when and
where they lived, Dickinson's poetry manifests an intrinsic literary
value; that is, she is both "soul of the age" and "for all time." If Anne
Bradstreet were a twentieth-century suburbanite rather than a
colonial housewife, her poems would be of interest only to her
friends. If Michael Wigglesworth were alive today, he would
probably be a televangelist rather than a poet. It is difficult to
imagine a civilization, however, in which "Because I could not stop
for Death" would not find at least a few responsive readers. In verse
that is derivative and not especially imaginative, though by no
means contemptible, Bradstreet states respectable (I mean the term
sincerely) commonplaces. From the commonplaces of her own

rather diminished world, Dickinson fashions a poetry that speaks to the essential human condition.

If we consider the two women as individuals, the life of the pioneer woman, Anne Bradstreet, is certainly richer and more capable of sustaining interest than that of Emily Dickinson, who spent most of her life as a recluse in her father's house in Amherst. To be sure, the conditions of Dickinson's life generate a good deal of attention from feminists nowadays; but, whatever the merits of this perspective, the revival of interest in her poetry preceded the rise of academic feminism, and it will surely outlast it—even as Sappho's poetry has survived 2,600 years of turmoil in literary and political fashion. While almost nothing is known about Sappho's life, there is still no doubt that the few fragments of her verse that have come down to us give her authentic canonical status as a poet. By the same token, Emily Dickinson's importance as a poet does not depend upon the circumstances of her life as a repressed, frustrated spinster in a "patriarchal" society—with all the grist thereby generated for the "dark satanic mills" of ideology.

Or perhaps I should say that Dickinson's biography is important because there is a repressed, frustrated spinster in all of us. To put it another way, it is part of the human condition to feel dependent, even helpless, unfulfilled, and at the mercy of what seems a senseless, arbitrary fate. The situation of an unmarried woman of Emily Dickinson's class in nineteenth-century New England can be taken as a special case of what is, ultimately, everyone's situation. We can all respond to her poems because she enjoys a unique perspective on what is an element pervasive in human life. Consider the particular instance of "Because I could not stop for Death"—we are all going to die. In the face of this inevitability, we all experience fear, hope, and just plain curiosity. Dickinson's poem draws upon a virgin's apprehensive yet fascinated imaginations of the wedding night: death is the ineluctable suitor who will have every maidenhead. This trope, which can be traced to the poet's own particular experience, converges with the broadly public symbolism of Christian tradition: all of us, men and women alike, are intended for brides of Christ; before God we are all feminine. Yet before that consummation devoutly to be wished, we must lie down in the marriage bed of the grave. The poem thus plays off the reassuring typology of the Bible (for example, the Song of Songs) against an individual's immediate perplexity and terror in order to dramatize a universal human ambivalence toward death.

But the power of the poem is not limited to a brilliant initial conception. A judicious selection and careful placement of every word, of every syllable, effect a tone of delicate irony, of subtle equivocation. The gossamer gown and tippet of tulle, cherished adornments of a diminutive, feminine world (and the kind of details that need explaining to undergraduates), enhance by contrast the stark, immense mystery of death. There is a delicious irony in the way the poem comments on its own not-quite-successful attempt to domesticate death: the tulle and gossamer prove inadequate, for "The Dews drew quivering and chill." Then there is the wry conceit that the grave is merely another "House," only it is almost completely buried: "The roof was scarcely visible— / The cornice—in the Ground." The startling appropriateness of "Cornice"—an architectural ornament that serves as a synecdoche for all the "useless" though precious details that enhance our lives—defies comment. It is matched by the use of "surmised" in the closing stanza:

> Since then—'tis Centuries—and yet
> Feels shorter than the Day
> I first surmised the Horses' Heads
> Were toward Eternity—

The poem as a whole is an evocation of all that is implied in this improbably perfect word, *surmised*: we are not told but reminded by way of an elusive verbal structure, delicate as the gossamer gown, that all our notions of death and "Eternity" lie in the realm of surmise.

There are various legitimate reasons for teaching a diversity of works in college classrooms, but at the heart of our curriculum should be the "canon"—a list of classic works that embody in a universally significant manner the common experience of men and women and enable us, by studying them, to grow into the full humanity that we share with others. Almost all the reasons for reading poetry are summed up in Cicero's *Pro Archia Poeta*, where the crafty lawyer promotes his old teacher's claim to Roman citizenship with every argument he can think of. Some of his reasons are practical: as an adult Cicero finds relief and relaxation for his "weary ears" after "the noise of the forum,"[18] and as a boy it was literary study that taught him that praise and honor only were worthy of pursuing with great effort in the face of every difficulty and danger. So his friends owe his success in defending them to poetry.[19] Some of his reasons border on vulgarity: Archias has celebrated Roman achievements in the past, and it is poetry that holds out the hope of future immortality for those now living.[20] But Cicero also perceives that poetry is valuable because of its intrinsic qualities. In a justly celebrated passage, he explains how literary education becomes a permanent part of the individual's inner life:

> Other occupations are not suitable for all times and places and ages; but these studies nourish youth and delight old age; they furnish the ornaments of prosperity and refuge and solace in adversity; they please at home without hindering us in public affairs; with us they pass long nights, lighten our journeys, and remain with us in the country.[21]

What the Greek and Latin writers have left us, Cicero explains, are "distinct models of gallant men, not only for contemplation, but even for imitation."[22] The key phrase here is "distinct models" (*imagines...expressas*); that is, models or figures or images finely crafted or shaped or squeezed out. If they are also for imitation, they are initially for contemplation; and indeed, that is *how* they are imitated, by assimilation into our souls—into our rational and imaginative being through study and contemplation. We teach such works because they help us to discern the order and purpose in human existence. It is a paradox of our nature that we must learn from others to be what we are, to attain authentic individual freedom. An acquaintance with great literature is certainly no substitute for character, but it enhances the moral imagination and is a good thing in itself. The most valuable educational service we can offer our students, as they strive to find themselves, is, in Matthew Arnold's still acute phrase, "*a disinterested endeavour to learn and propagate the best that is known and thought in the world.*"[23]

Notes

CHAPTER ONE

1. John Crowe Ransom, *The World's Body* (1938; rpt. Baton Rouge: Louisiana State University Press, 1968), is a seminal collection of essays by a founding figure of the New Criticism. It was Ransom's *The New Criticism* (New York: New Directions, 1941) that probably is responsible for establishing the identification between the term and the close reading of texts, although Edwin Berry Burgum, ed., *The New Criticism: An Anthology of Modern Aesthetic and Literary Criticism* (New York: Prentice-Hall, 1930) uses the title earlier, taking it from a reprinted essay by J.E. Spingarn (pp. 3-25). Cleanth Brooks and Robert Penn Warren, *Understanding Poetry* (New York: Holt, 1938), was an extremely influential anthology of poems and introduction to the close critical reading of poetry. It provided the model for numerous similar textbooks of which Laurence J. Perrine, *Sound and Sense* (New York: Harcourt, Brace & World, 1956), was one of the most successful.

2. "The New Criticism: Pro and Contra," in *The Attack on Literature and Other Essays* (Chapel Hill: University of North Carolina Press, 1982), p. 87.

3. *Irony's Edge: The Theory and Politics of Irony* (London and New York: Routledge, 1994), pp. 2, 94, 176-204 passim.

4. Ibid., pp. 144-45.

5. Ibid., pp. 12-13.

6. "Irony as a Principle of Structure," in *Literary Opinion in America*, ed. Morton Dauwen Zabel (3rd ed., New York: Harper & Row, 1962), II, 740.

7. *Echoes of Desire: English Petrarchism and Its Counterdiscourses* (Ithaca and London: Cornell University Press, 1995), p. 247.

8. *The Attack on Literature*, p. 87.

9. *The Pursuit of Signs: Semiotics, Literature, Deconstruction* (Ithaca, NY: Cornell University Press, 1981), pp. 3, 5.

10. Ibid., p. 6.

11. Ibid., p. 12.

12. *The Crisis in Criticism: Theory, Literature, and Reform in English Studies* (Baltimore and London: Johns Hopkins University Press, 1984), p. 101.

13. Ibid., p. 105.

14. Ibid., pp. 110-11. It is worth noting that the specific object of Cain's reproof here is Helen Vendler, hardly someone who could be called a "conservative."

15. Ibid., p. 116.

16. Ibid., p. 255.

17. Ibid., p. 265. See pp. 247-77 passim.

18. *Literature Lost: Social Agendas and the Corruption of the Humanities* (New Haven and London: Yale University Press, 1997), pp. 8-9.

19. See Allen Bloom, *The Closing of the American Mind* (New York: Simon & Schuster,1987); E.D. Hirsch, *Cultural Literacy: What Every American Needs to Know* (Boston: Houghton Mifflin, 1987); *The Dissolution of General Education: 1914-1993* (Princeton, NJ: National Association of Scholars, 1996). For a recent account of Stanley Fish's attack on the NAS as an organization "widely known to be racist, sexist, and homophobic," see Ellis, *Literature Lost*, p. 245, n. 11.

20. *Irony's Edge*, p. 97.

21. *The New Science of Politics: An Introduction*, foreword Dante Germino (1952; rpt. Chicago and London: University of Chicago Press, 1987), pp. 107-61.

22. *Confessionum S. Augustini* VII. *Patrologia Latina* 32.733-48. Elaine Pagels, *The Gnostic Gospels* (1979; rpt. New York: Vintage Books, 1981), pp. 171-74.

23. For a sympathetic account of the Marxist interpretation of society and literature in terms of "base" and "superstructure," see Terry Eagleton, *Marxism and Literary Criticism* (Berkeley and Los Angeles: University of California Press, 1976), pp. 3-19. For a contemporary Gnostic literary theorist, see Harold Bloom, *Agon: Towards a Theory of Revisionism* (New York and Oxford: Oxford University Press, 1982), esp. p. 78: "...if you are not to be hedged in by God's incomprehensible power, then you must dissent from the doctrine of Creation. You must learn to speculate about the origins, and the aim of your speculation will have to be a vision of catastrophe, for only a divine catastrophe will allow for your own, your human freedom." See also Ihab Hassan, "The New Gnosticism: Speculations on an Aspect of the Postmodern Mind," in *Paracriticisms: Seven Speculations of the Times* (Urbana, Chicago, London: University of Illinois Press, 1975), pp. 121-47.

24. *Literature Lost*, p. 119.

25. Gerald Graff, *Literature Against Itself: Literary Ideas in Modern Society* (Chicago and London: University of Chicago Press, 1979), correctly asserts, "Most theories of the nature of literature are more or less concealed theories of the nature of man and of the good society. In this sense, literary thinking is inseparable from moral and social thinking" (p. 1); however, as the remainder of this chapter seeks to show, he is in error in a subsequent assertion that "the key principle of the New Criticism...[is] its hostile (or at best equivocal) view of the referential powers of literature" (p. 6), if by "referential" he intends (as context suggests) "representational" or "mimetic."

26. A notable reason for the qualification "almost all" would be I.A. Richards, *Principles of Literary Criticism* (New York: Harcourt, Brace & World, 1925), pp. 81-91,113, 261-

87, who assumes a logical positivist outlook and regards poems as vehicles of "emotive meaning" useful for "ordering the impulses" of human beings in contrast to scientific "referential meaning."

27. The most concise and accessible account is René Wellek and Austin Warren, "The Mode of Existence of a Literary Work of Art," in *Theory of Literature* (3rd ed., New York: Harcourt, Brace & World, 1956), pp. 142-57. Wellek and Warren draw substantially on the treatment by Roman Ingarden, *The Literary Work of Art: An Investigation on the Borderlines of Ontology, Logic, and Theory of Literature*, trans. George G. Grabowicz (Evanston, IL: Northwestern University Press, 1973), esp. pp. 356-64. The critical implications are dealt with in classic essays by W.K. Wimsatt, Jr., and Monroe C. Beardsley, "The Intentional Fallacy" and "The Affective Fallacy," in *The Verbal Icon: Studies in the Meaning of Poetry* (Lexington: University of Kentucky Press, 1954), pp. 3-39.

28. *The Gnostic Gospels*, p. 135.

29. Ibid., pp. 148, 149.

30. The key book is *Anatomy of Criticism: Four Essays* (Princeton, NJ: Princeton University Press, 1957), see esp. "Anagogic Phase: Symbol as Monad," pp. 115-28. W. K. Wimsatt, "Northrop Frye: Criticism as Myth," in *The Day of the Leopards: Essays in Defense of Poems* (New Haven and London: Yale University Press, 1976), p. 74, designates Frye's theory as "Gnostic mythopoeia."

31. *The Attack on Literature*, pp. 3ff.

32. *Cultural Literacy*, pp. 21-26.

33. *The Attack on Literature*, p. 12.

34. "Education" ultimately derives from the Latin *educere*, "to lead forth" or "out" (*ex-*). See the *Oxford English Dictionary*, s.v. "educate" and the *Oxford Latin Dictionary*, s.v. "educo." For Plato's "Cave" see the *Republic* VII.514A-520E.

35. *The Historical Renaissance: New Essays on Tudor and Stuart Literature and Culture* (Chicago and London: University of Chicago Press, 1988), pp. 1-2, 3.

36. *Criticism and Social Change* (Chicago: University of Chicago Press, 1984), p. 152.

37. *Is There a Text in This Class? The Authority of Interpretive Communities* (Cambridge, MA: Harvard University Press, 1980), p. 368.

38. *The Well Wrought Urn: Studies in the Structure of Poetry* (New York: Harcourt, Brace & World, 1947), pp. x-xi. Toward the end of his life, Brooks published *Historical Evidence and the Reading of Seventeenth-Century Poetry* (Columbia and London: University of Missouri Press, 1991), which makes detailed forays into the historical context of a number of poems.

39. Donne's poetry is quoted from *The Complete Poetry of John Donne*, ed. John T. Shawcross (Garden City, NY: Doubleday & Co., 1967). Line numbers are given parenthetically in the text.

40. *The Well Wrought Urn*, p. 16.

41. *Metaphoric Worlds: Conceptions of a Romantic Nature* (New Haven and London: Yale University Press, 1988), p. 3.

42. *The Well Wrought Urn*, p. 17.

43. *On Deconstruction: Theory and Criticism After Structuralism* (Ithaca, NY: Cornell University Press, 1982), pp.201-04.

44. *An Apology for Poetry,* in *Elizabethan Critical Essays,* ed. G. Gregory Smith (London: Oxford University Press, 1904), I, 185.
45. Culler, *On Deconstruction,* p. 205.

CHAPTER TWO

1. *There's No Such Thing as Free Speech and It's a Good Thing, Too* (New York and Oxford: Oxford University Press, 1994), p. 57.
2. *Loose Canons: Notes on the Culture Wars* (New York and Oxford: Oxford University Press, 1992), pp. 35-36
3. "The Critic as Host," in *Deconstruction and Criticism* (New York: Seabury, 1979), pp. 223, 226.
4. *Course in General Linguistics,* trans. Wade Baskin (1959; rpt. New York: McGraw-Hill, 1966), p. 118.
5. See Fredric Jameson, *The Prison-House of Language: A Critical Account of Structuralism and Russian Formalism* (Princeton, NJ: Princeton University Press, 1972); see also Hillis Miller, "The Critic as Host," p. 230: "We have no other language. The language of criticism is subject to exactly the same limitations and blind alleys as the works it reads. The most heroic effort to escape from the prison-house of language only builds the walls higher."
6. *Speech and Phenomena and Other Essays on Husserl's Theory of Signs,* trans. David B. Allison (Evanston, IL: Northwestern University Press, 1973), p. 65.
7. *Of Grammatology,* trans. Gayatri Chakravorty Spivak (Baltimore and London: Johns Hopkins University Press, 1976), p. 71.
8. *Against Deconstruction* (Princeton, NJ: Princeton University Press, 1989), pp. 151, 96. See also Raymond Tallis, *Not Saussure: A Critique of Post-Saussurean Literary Theory* (2nd ed., New York: St. Martin's Press, 1995), for an even more devastating attack on the linguistic and philosophic pretensions of deconstruction and postmodernism generally.
9. This has been amply witnessed by the reassessment of feminism by Christina Hoff Sommers, *Who Stole Feminism? How Women Have Betrayed Women* (New York: Simon & Schuster, 1994); and Elizabeth Fox-Genovese, *Feminism Is Not the Story of My Life: How Today's Feminist Elite Has Lost Touch with the Real Concerns of Women* (New York: Nan A. Talese, 1996), to name only two of the most prominent accounts.
10. *The World, the Text, and the Critic* (Cambridge, MA: Harvard University Press, 1983), p. 214.
11. *After the New Criticism* (Chicago: University of Chicago Press, 1980), p. 177. See also the nagging questions of Guy Scarpetta and Jean-Louis Houdebine in *Positions,* trans. Alan Bass (Chicago: University of Chicago Press, 1980), pp. 56, 60-62, 67-68, 79-81, 88-89, in which the two interviewers, especially the latter, try unsuccessfully to elicit from Derrida an affirmation of Marxist dialectic and its exemption from the deconstructive process.
12. *Confessions* IV.1, *Patrologia Latina* 32.693: "Et quis homo est quilibet homo, cum sit homo?"

13. Ibid. IV.10, *Patrologia* 32.699: "Tantum dedisti eis, quia partes sunt rerum, quae non sunt omnes simul; sed decedendo ac succedendo agunt omnes universum, cujus partes sunt. Ecce sic peragitur et sermo noster per signa sonantia. Non enim erit totus sermo, si unum verbum non decedat cum sonuerit partes suas, ut succedat aliud."

14. Ibid. XI.7, *Patrologia* 32.812-13: "Neque enim finitur quod dicebatur, et dicitur aliud ut possint dici omnia; sed simul ac sempiterne omnia. Alioquin jam tempus et mutatio, et non vera aeternitas, nec vera immortalitas."

15. *Speech and Phenomena*, p. 65.

16. *De Trinitate* IV.30, *Patrologia Latina* 42. 909-10: "Sed plane fidenter dixerim, Patrem et Filium et Spiritum sanctum unius ejusdemque substantiae, Deum creatorem, Trinitatem omnipotentem inseparabiliter operari: sed ita non posse per longe imparem maximeque corpoream creaturam inseparabiliter demonstrari; sicut per voces nostras, quae utique corporaliter sonant, non possunt Pater et Filius et Spiritus sanctus, nisi suis et propriis intervallis temporum certa separatione distinctis, quae suae cujusque vocabuli syllabae occupant, nominari. In sua quippe substantia sunt, tria unum sunt, Pater et Filius et Spiritus sanctus, nullo temporali motu super omnem creaturam idipsum sine ullis intervallis temporum vel locorum, et simul unum atque idem ab aeternitate in aeternitatem, tanquam ipsa aeternitas quae sine veritate et charitate non est: in meis autem vocibus separati sunt Pater et Filius et Spiritus sanctus, nec simul dici potuerunt, et in litteris visibilibus sua separatim locorum spatia tenuerunt. Et quemadmodum cum memoriam meam et intellectum et voluntatem nomino, singula quidem nomina ad res singulas referuntur, sed tamen ab omnibus tribus singula facta sunt; nullum enim horum trium nominum est, quod non et memoria et intellectus et voluntas mea simul operata sint: ita Trinitas simul operata est et vocem Patris, et carnem Filii, et columbam Spiritus sancti, cum ad personas singulas singula haec referantur."

17. "Différance," in *Margins of Philosophy*, trans. Alan Bass (Chicago: University of Chicago Press, 1982), p. 6.

18. Ibid., p. 26.

19. Ibid., pp. 26-27.

20. *Speech and Phenomena*, p. 53.

21. Ibid., p. 54.

22. *Confessions* XI.14; *Patrologia Latina* 32.816: "Duo ergo illa tempora, praeteritum et futurum quomodo sunt, quando et praeteritum jam non est, et futurum nondum est? Praesens autem si semper esset praesens, nec in praeteritum transiret; jam non esset tempus, sed aeternitas. Si ergo praesens, ut tempus sit, ideo fit quia in praeteritum transit; quomodo et hoc esse dicimus, cui causa ut sit illa est, quia non erit; ut scilicet non vere dicamus tempus esse, nisi quia tendit non esse?"

23. *Speech and Phenomena*, pp. 103, 104.

24. Kant lays the groundwork for Derrida by radically subjectivizing metaphysical knowledge. See, for instance, Immanuel Kant, *Prolegomena to Any Future Metaphysics*, trans. Paul Carus (1902; rpt. LaSalle, IL: Open Court, 1967), p. 80: "The possibility of experience in general is therefore at the same time the universal law of nature, and the principles of the experience are the very laws of nature. For we do not know nature but as the totality of appearances, i.e., of representations in us, and hence we

can only derive the laws of its connexion from the principles of their connexion in us, that is, from the conditions of their necessary union in consciousness, which constitutes the possibility of experience." Once human consciousness and discourse of reason are shown to be captive to the arbitrary set of signifiers that constitute language, then the last site of "presence" undergirding the "representations" disappears.

25. St. Augustine makes the same point about doubt; to doubt is "to know that one does not know," and this knowledge is a certainty. See *De Trinitate* X.14, *Patrologia Latina* 42.981: "...si dubitat, scit se nescire; si dubitat, judicat non se temere consentire oportere. Quisquis igitur aliunde dubitat, de his omnibus dubitare non debet: quae si non essent, de ulla re dubitare non posset."

26. *Confessions* XI.31; *Patrologia Latina* 32.826: "Longe tu, longe mirabilius, longeque secretius. Neque enim sicut nota cantantis notumve canticum audientis, expectatione vocum futurarum et memoria praeteritarum variatur affectus, sensusque distenditur; ita tibi aliquid accidit incommutabiliter aeterno, hoc est, vere creatori mentium. Sicut ergo nosti in principio coelum et terram sine varietate notitiae tuae, ita fecisti in principio coelum et terram sine distentione actionis tuae. Qui intelligit, confiteatur tibi; et qui non intelligit, confiteatur tibi." *Confiteatur tibi* is usually rendered, "Let him praise you." The verb *confiteor*, which means both to "confess" or "avow" and to "praise," provides the root idea of Augustines's title, *Confessions*. I have used the verb "acknowledge" because it seems to combine the notions of confessing and praising. Except for the violation of longstanding tradition, the title might well be translated "Acknowledgements."

27. "Structure, Sign, and Play in the Discourse of the Human Sciences," in *The Structuralist Controversy: The Languages of Criticism and the Sciences of Man*, ed. Richard Macksey and Eugenio Donato (Baltimore and London: Johns Hopkins University Press, 1970), p. 250.

28. "Metaphysics as Tarbaby: Intention, Deconstruction, and Absolutes," *Center Journal* 1 (1982), No. 2: 29.

29. *Margins*, p. 6.

30. *Derrida on the Mend* (West Lafayette, IN: Purdue University Press, 1984), p. 18.

31. *Margins*, p. 258.

32. *De Veritate* ii.11; *Quaestiones Disputatae* XI (5th ed.,Turin and Rome: Marietti, 1927), III, 59. The following is the entire passage that I have excerpted and paraphrased: "Quidquid autem est in Deo, hoc est suum proprium esse; sicut enim essentia in eo est idem quod esse, ita scientia idem est quod scientem esse in eo; unde, cum esse quod est proprium unius rei non possit alteri communicari, impossibile est quod creatura pertingat ad eamdem rationem habendi aliquid quod habet Deus, sicut impossibile est quod ad idem esse perveniat. Similiter etiam in nobis esset: si enim in Petro non differret homo et hominem esse, impossibile esset quod homo univoce diceretur de Petro et Paulo, quibus est esse diversum; nec tamen potest dici quod omnino aequivoce praedicetur quidquid de Deo et creatura dicitur, quia si non esset aliqua convenientia creaturae ad Deum secundum rem, sua essentia non esset creaturarum similitudo; et ita cognoscendo essentiam suam non cognosceret creaturas. Similiter etiam nec nos ex rebus creatis in cognitionem Dei pervenire possemus; nec

nominum quae creaturis aptantur, unum magis de eo dicendum esset quam aliud; quia ex aequivocis non differt quodcumque nomen imponatur, ex quo nulla rei convenientia attenditur. Unde dicendum est, quod nec omnino univoce, nec pure aequivoce, nomen scientiae de scientia Dei et nostra praedicatur; sed secundum analogiam, quod nihil est aliud dictu quam secundum proportionem."

33. *Confessions* VI.8; *Patrologia Latina* 32.726: "Et non erat jam ille qui venerat, sed unus de turba ad quam venerat, et verus eorum socius, a quibus adductus erat."

34. *Convergences to the Source of Christian Mystery*, trans. E.A. Nelson (San Francisco: Ignatius Press, 1983), p. 14.

35. Ibid., p. 129. See Augustine *De Trinitate* XII.16; *Patrologia Latina* 42.1007i: "In what way did he [man] pass so far from the heights to the depths except through the middle of himself" ("Qua igitur tam longe transiret a summis ad infima, nisi per medium sui?").

36. *Signs of the Times: Deconstruction and the Fall of Paul de Man* (New York: Poseidon Press, 1991), pp. 108-09.

37. For the definitive statement of the argument, see Stanley L. Jaki, *The Road of Science and the Ways to God* (Chicago: University of Chicago Press, 1978).

38. C. S. Lewis and E.M.W. Tillyard, *The Personal Heresy* (London: Oxford University Press, 1939), p. 97.

39. *Derrida on the Mend*, p. 35. See also p. 45.

40. For the Patristic origin of the doctrine of the Real Presence, see Jaroslav Pelikan, *The Christian Tradition: A History of the Development of Doctrine*, Vol I., *The Emergence of the Catholic Tradition (100-600)* (Chicago and London: University of Chicago Press, 1971), pp. 166-69. I paraphrase the doctrine in its strongest Roman Catholic form, but some sense of Real Presence in the Eucharist is important to the Eastern Orthodox, Lutheran, and Anglican traditions of Christianity as well.

41. Henr. Denzinger et Clem. Bannwart, S.J., *Enchiridion Symbolorum, Definitionum et Declarationum* (17th ed., Friburgi Brigoviae: Herder, 1928), #695: "Illa [sacramenta antiquae Legis] enim non causabant gratiam, sed eam solum per passionem Christi dandam esse figurabant; haec vero nostra [Novae Legis sacramenta] et continent gratiam, et ipsam digne suscipientibus conferunt." See also #849.

42. Ibid., #874: "Principio docet sancta Synodus et aperte ac simpliciter profitetur, in almo sanctae Eucharistiae sacramento post panis et vini consecrationem Dominum nostrum Iesum Christum verum Deum atque hominem vere realiter ac substantialiter sub specie illarum rerum sensibilium contineri."

43. For Derrida's interest in the Judaic overtones of his own thought, see "Edmond Jabès and the Question of the Book" and "Violence and Metaphysics: An Essay on the Thought of Emmanuel Levinas," chapters 3 and 4 of *Writing and Difference*, trans. Alan Bass (Chicago: University of Chicago Press, 1978), pp. 64-153.

44. For an effort to salvage some kind of religious affirmation from deconstruction, see Mark C. Taylor, *Erring: A Postmodern A/theology* (Chicago and London: University of Chicago Press, 1984).

45. Quoted by Lehman, *Signs of the Times*, p. 143. I am indebted to Lehman's account for the factual information about the de Man affair in this paragraph.

46. See Jacques Derrida, "Like the Sound of the Sea Deep within a Shell," *Critical Inquiry*

14 (1988): 591-652; and the equally impenitent Barbara Johnson in "A Note on the Wartime Writings of Paul de Man," the preface to the paperback edition of *A World of Difference* (Baltimore and London: Johns Hopkins University Press, 1989), pp. xi-xviii. Such turgidly written and flimsily reasoned defenses of de Man are justly and ferociously shredded by David H. Hirsch, *The Deconstruction of Literature: Criticism After Auschwitz* (Hanover, NH, and London: University Press of New England, 1991) esp. pp. 69-117.

47. *Signs of the Times*, p. 267.

48. This and the following quotations from "A Good Man Is Hard to Find" are taken from Flannery O'Connor, *Collected Works*, ed. Sally Fitzgerald (New York: Library of America, 1988), pp. 152-53. For O'Connor's own very incisive comments on the story, see "On Her Own Work," in Flannery O'Connor, *Mystery and Manners*, ed. Sally and Robert Fitzgerald (New York: Farrar, Strauss & Giroux, 1966), pp. 107-14.

49. "Dissemination" is the fourth, title essay of Jacques Derrida's *Dissemination*, trans. Barbara Johnson (Chicago: University of Chicago Press, 1981), pp. 287-329.

CHAPTER THREE

1. *The Genealogy of Morals* XIII, in *The Birth of Tragedy and the Genealogy of Morals*, trans. Francis Golffing (Garden City, NY: Doubleday & Co., 1966), pp. 178-79.

2. *Genealogy* XXIV, p. 287.

3. I would therefore differ with John Ellis, *Against Deconstruction* (Princeton, NJ: Princeton University Press, 1989), pp. 35-38, who seems to me to make a strategic error in accepting Derrida's reductivist view of what the term "logocentric" can properly mean. Cf. Ewa M. Thompson, "Dialectical Methodologies in the American Academy," *Modern Age* 28 (1984), No. 1, 10-11, for a more useful view of the place of logocentric thinking in the Western tradition.

4. "Structure, Sign, and Play in the Discourse of the Human Sciences," in *The Structuralist Controversy: The Languages of Criticism and the Sciences of Man*, ed. Richard Macksey and Eugenio Donato (Baltimore and London: Johns Hopkins University Press, 1970), p. 249. See above Chap. 2, p. 52, n. 35, for St. Augustine's assertion that man falls into the depths (*infima*) by trying to find his center (*medium*) in himself.

5. Ibid., p. 250. Emphasis in original. See above Chap. 2, p. 48, and p. 170, n. 27.

6. *The Abolition of Man* (1947; rpt. New York: Collier Books, 1962), pp. 77-78.

7. "Introduction" to *The Poetical Works of Shelley* (New York: Thomas Crowell, n.d.), pp. 1-2.

8. Ibid., p. 4.

9. "Shelley Disfigured," in, *Deconstruction and Criticism* (New York: Seabury Press, 1979), pp. 67, 68.

10. Ibid., pp. 67, 68-69. See the chapter on de Man in Stephen W. Melville, *Philosophy Beside Itself: On Deconstruction and Modernism*, foreword Donald Marshall (Minneapolis: University of Minnesota Press, 1986), pp. 115-38, esp. p. 135, on de Man's distaste for "[M.H.] Abrams' acceptance of a sharp, theologically patterned break between modernism and romanticism."

11. Paul de Man, "Criticism and Crisis," in *Blindness and Insight: Essays on Contemporary Rhetoric*, intro. Wlad Godzich, (2nd rev. ed., Minneapolis: University of Minnesota Press, 1983), p. 12.

12. Ibid., pp. 17, 18. See Melville, p. 137: "Its [criticism's] task is above all to know—to force the knowledge of—that which we would mostly deny: the literature that names our nothingness and our isolation, the weight of our freedom." See also William Ray, *Literary Meaning: From Phenomenology to Deconstruction* (Oxford: Basil Blackwell, 1984), p. 199, who remarks that de Man's theory "requires that he demonstrate the fallacy of correlating action with subject—that he show a performative side of language not dependent on the intervention of a meaningful act." De Man's work thus suggests that what usually gets deconstructed is the autonomy of the conscious subject of the Enlightenment's purely secular humanism: the individual cannot guarantee the stability of his own meaning, cannot, that is, be his own Logos.

13. "Good Country People," in *Collected Works*, ed. Sally Fitzgerald (New York: Library of America, 1988), p. 280.

14. *Confessions* I.1, *Patrologia Latina* 32.661: "fecisti nos ad te, et inquietum est cor nostrum, donec requiescat in te."

15. Sancti Thomas Aquinitatis, *De Veritate Catholicae Fidei Contra Gentiles* III.37, 2nd ed. I. Bertrand (Paris: Bloud et Barral, 1882), p. 300: "quod ultima felicitas hominis non consistit nisi in contemplatione Dei."

16. "The Breaking of Form," in *Deconstruction and Criticism*, pp. 3-4, 5-6.

17. Ibid., p. 16.

18. *The Breaking of the Vessels* (Chicago: University of Chicago Press, 1982), p. 29.

19. "The Breaking of Form," p. 9.

20. *The Breaking of the Vessels*, p. 29.

21. Ibid., p. 40.

22. Ibid., p. 69.

23. Ibid., p. 13.

24. This and the following passages of the poem are quoted from Wallace Stevens, *The Palm at the End of the Mind: Selected Poems and a Play*, ed. Holly Stevens (New York: Random House, 1972), p. 367.

25. M. H. Abrams, *Natural Supernaturalism: Tradition and Revolution in Romantic Literature* (New York: W.W. Norton & Co., 1971).

26. *The Breaking of the Vessels*, p. 105. Bloom's interpretation in this volume is basically a reprise of an earlier treatment in *Wallace Stevens: The Poems of Our Climate* (Ithaca and London: Cornell University Press, 1977), pp. 354-59.

27. Ibid., p.107.

28. On Stevens' conversion see Peter Brazeau, *Parts of a World: Wallace Stevens Remembered: An Oral Biography* (New York: Random House, 1983), pp. 294-97; and Joan Richardson, *Wallace Stevens: The Later Years, 1923-1955* (New York: William Morrow, 1988), pp. 426-27. The evidence of the conversion is overwhelming, although Stevens' daughter rejected the idea persistently.

29. Jacques Lacan, "The Meaning of the Phallus," in *Feminine Sexuality: Jacques Lacan and the école freudienne*, ed. Juliet Mitchell & Jacqueline Rose, trans. Jacqueline Rose (New York: W.W. Norton & Co., 1985), p. 79.

30. *De civitate Dei* 7.21. *Patrologia Latina* 41.210-11: "Cui membro inhonesto matremfamilias honestissimam palam coronam necesse erat imponere."

31. Jan Miel, "Jacques Lacan and the Structure of the Unconscious," in *Structuralism*, ed. Jacques Ehrmann (Garden City, NY: Doubleday Anchor, 1970), p. 98.

32. Lacan, "The Meaning of the Phallus," p. 82.

33. Raman Selden, *A Reader's Guide to Contemporary Literary Theory* (Lexington: University Press of Kentucky, 1985), p. 143.

34. "Introduction—I," in *Feminine Sexuality*, p. 11.

35. "Introduction—II," in *Feminine Sexualilty*, p. 45.

36. "The Meaning of the Phallus," pp. 81-82.

37. Rose, "Introduction—II," p. 30.

38. Lacan, "Seminar of 21 January 1975," in *Feminine Sexuality*, p. 165. See the exposition of Lacan by Melville, *Philosophy Beside Itself*, esp. p. 63: "The infant comes to itself in alienation, in slippage against itself and as other than whole."

39. Jacques Lacan, "Of Structure as an Inmixing of an Otherness Prerequisite to Any Subject Whatsoever," in *The Structuralist Controversy*, ed. Macksey and Donato, p. 194.

40. See Melville, pp. 84-114; and Jonathan Culler, *On Deconstruction: Theory and Criticism After Structuralism* (Ithaca, NY: Cornell University Press, 1982), p. 27n; and Barbara Johnson, "The Frame of Reference: Poe, Lacan, Derrida," in *Psychoanalysis and the Question of the Text*, ed. Geoffrey H. Hartman (Baltimore and London: Johns Hopkins University Press, 1978), pp. 149-71.

41. "God and the *Jouissance* of The Woman: A Love Letter," in *Feminine Sexuality*, pp. 140, 147.

42. "The Meaning of the Phallus," p. 80.

43. *Reading Lacan* (Ithaca, NY, and London: Cornell University Press, 1985), pp. 159-60.

44. Ibid., p. 85.

45. "Preface" to *Psychoanalysis and the Question of the Text*, ed. Geoffrey H. Hartman (Baltimore and London: Johns Hopkins University Press, 1978), p. vii.

46. "The Frame of Reference: Poe, Lacan, Derrida," in *Psychoanalysis and the Question of the Text*, p. 153. The italics, brackets, and ellipsis are in Johnson's original text. I have omitted a bracketed citation of Derrida.

47. Ibid., p. 158.

48. Ibid., p. 170. Italics in original, bracketed phrase interpolated.

49. Ibid., p. 154.

50. "'Too Beautiful Altogether': Patriarchal Ideology in *Heart of Darkness*," in Ross C. Murfin, ed., *Heart of Darkness: A Case Study in Contemporary Criticism* (New York: St. Martin's Press, 1989), p. 180.

51. "Introduction—II," *Feminine Sexuality*, p. 27.

CHAPTER FOUR

1. Thomas Hobbes, *Leviathan* I.11, ed. C.B. MacPherson (Harmondsworth: Penguin Books, 1968), pp. 160-61.

2. Ibid., I.10, 151-52.

3. *The Order of Things: An Archaeology of the Human Sciences* (1970; rpt. New York: Vintage Books, 1973), p. xiv.

4. Ibid., p. xxii.

5. Ibid., p. xxiii.

6. "What Is an Author?" in *The Foucault Reader*, ed. Paul Rabinow (New York: Random House, 1984), p. 110.

7. Ibid., p. 118.

8. Ibid., p. 119. For Wordsworth, see "Preface" to *Lyrical Ballads*, in *The Prose Works of William Wordsworth*, ed. A.B. Grosart (London, 1876), II, 87.

9. *After the New Criticism* (Chicago: University of Chicago Press, 1980), p. 196. For a later reflection by Lentricchia on the relationship between Marx and Foucault, and their joint influence on the New Historicism, see "Michel Foucault's Fantasy for Humanists," in *Ariel and the Police: Michel Foucault, William James, Wallace Stevens* (Madison: University of Wisconsin Press, 1988), pp. 29-102.

10. Ibid., pp. 197-98.

11. Ibid., p. 199. In *Ariel and the Police*, Lentricchia asks rueful questions about the negative implications of Foucault's notion of discourse for affirmative Marxist social change, such as the following, p. 31: "In spite of his own work in French prisons, does Foucault's theory of power, and his account of the emergence of modern society, constitute, however unwittingly, a testament of despair?"

12. Ibid., p. 201.

13. Ibid., pp. 208-09.

14. "Anatomy of a Jar," in *Ariel and the Police*, pp. 4-5.

15. Ibid., pp. 22, 20-21. For the political impression left by Stevens among acquaintances and associates, see Peter Brazeau, *Parts of a World: Wallace Stevens Remembered: An Oral Biography* (New York: Random House, 1983), pp. 123, 144, 149-50, 153, 277-78. For an effort to give a nuanced view of Stevens' conservatism, see Joan Richardson, *Wallace Stevens: The Later Years, 1923-1955* (New York: William Morrow, 1988), pp. 108-13, 338-39.

16. "Anecdote of the Jar," is quoted from *The Collected Poems of Wallace Stevens* (New York: Alfred Knopf, 1954), p. 56.

17. *Ariel and the Police*, p. 16.

18. Ibid., pp. 19-20.

19. See Frank Lentricchia, "Last Will and Testament of an Ex-Literary Critic," *Lingua Franca* (September/October 1996), pp. 59-67, for a kind of palinode where Lentricchia confesses that he teaches his undergraduate classes with the premise "that literature is important as literature," a notion which provokes knowing laughs among graduate students (p. 60).

20. *Renaissance Self-Fashioning from More to Shakespeare* (Chicago and London: University of Chicago Press, 1980).

21. *Chaste Thinking: The Rape of Lucretia and the Birth of Humanism* (Bloomington and Indianapolis: Indiana University Press, 1989), p. 2.

22. Ibid., pp. 5, 7.

23. Debora Shuger, "Castigating Livy: The Rape of Lucretia and *The Old Arcadia*,"

Renaissance Quarterly 51 (1998): pp. 526-48, demonstrates that Jed herself gets the philology wrong, because *castus* and *castigare* are etymologically related to castration and hence refer directly to male, rather than female, chastity: "Jed's tendentious philology simply erases the fact that, from antiquity through the Renaissance, 'chaste thinking' regularly concerned issues of male purity, of the (violent) constraints placed on male sexuality, of the need to control male bodies" (530). Debora Shuger is one of the best of a number of contemporary literary scholars, to whom the label "New Historicist" is often attached, doing judicious and often brilliant work. My strictures are aimed only at New Historicism as an ideology.

24. *Chaste Thinking*, p. 8.

25. Ibid., pp. 48-49.

26. Ibid., p. 33.

27. A further tacit implication of Jed's notion of "chaste thinking" is that, just as there is no difference between scribal error and philological emendation, even so there is no difference between Tarquin's rape of Lucretia and Collatinus' marital intercourse with her. Several times Jed cites Catherine MacKinnon, who is notorious for maintaining that all heterosexual intercourse is equivalent to rape.

28. Virgil, *Eclogues*, ed. and trans. Guy Lee (rev. ed., Harmondsworth: Penguin Books, 1984), p. 123.

29. *Shakespeare Reproduced: The Text in History and Ideology* (New York and London: Methuen, 1987), p. 3.

30. Ibid., p. 2.

31. Ibid., p. 3.

32. *Republic* 516c-e.

33. *Shakespeare Reproduced*, pp. 3-4.

34. *Shakespeare's Doctrine of Nature: A Study of King Lear* (London: Faber and Faber, 1948), p. 15.

35. *Shakespeare Reproduced*, pp. 4-5.

36. Ibid., p. 5.

37. Ibid., p. 8.

38. Ibid., p. 9.

39. Ibid., p. 8.

40. Ibid., p. 101.

41. Ibid., p. 104.

42. Ibid., p. 105.

43. Ibid., p. 107.

44. Ibid.

45. Ibid., p. 112

46. Stanley Wells, Introduction to *The Tempest*, in William Shakespeare, *The Complete Works: Compact Edition*, ed. Stanley Wells et al (Oxford: Clarendon Press, 1988), p. 1167.

47. *Things of Darkness: Economies of Race and Gender in Early Modern England* (Ithaca, NY, and London: Cornell University Press, 1995), p. 142.

48. Ibid., pp. 150-51.

49. Ibid., p. 148.

50. "Fiction and Friction," in *Shakespearean Negotiations: The Circulation of Social Energy in Renaissance England* (Berkeley and Los Angeles: University of California Press, 1988), p. 75.

51. Ibid., pp. 92-93.

52. "Individual and Historical Process in *King Lear*," in David Aers, Bob Hodge, and Gunther Kress, *Language and Society in England, 1580-1680* (Totowa, NJ: Barnes & Noble, 1981), p. 88.

53. Ibid., pp. 87, 88.

54. Ibid., pp. 93-94, 98-99.

55. Ibid., p. 94.

CHAPTER FIVE

1. For the background and response to Meese's speech, see J.P. McFadden, "Introduction," and Joseph Sobran, "Abortion, the Court and Federalism," both in *The Human Life Review* 12 (1986), No. 1, 2-3, 17-18, respectively. The quotations from Justice Brennan are taken from Raoul Berger, "Justice Brennan Is Wrong," as reprinted in the same issue of *HLR*, pp. 106-08, originally published in the New York *Times* Op-Ed Page, 28 October 1985.

2. On 21 October 1986, Meese maintained, in a speech given at Tulane University, that the Constitution itself, not Supreme Court rulings, is the "supreme law of the land." See the Raleigh *News & Observer*, 23 October 1986. By November, 1986, the attention of Meese and the administration was diverted by the Republican midterm electoral debacle and the disclosure of covert arms dealings involving Iran and Nicaraguan Contras.

3. "Justice Brennan Is Wrong," p. 106.

4. "Forgotten Checks and Balances," *The Human Life Review* 12 (1986), No. 1, 104; first released by the Universal Press Syndicate, 12 November 1985.

5. Catherine Belsey, *Critical Practice* (London and New York: Methuen, 1980), p. 36. I am quoting the fourth printing of 1986. Terence Hawkes's comment in the "General Editor's Preface" is worth noting: "Each volume in the series will seek to encourage rather than resist the process of change, to stretch rather than resist the boundaries that currently define literature and its academic study." Change per se is thus a desideratum.

6. *St. Thomas Aquinas* (1933), *The Collected Works of G.K. Chesterton*, ed. George J. Marlin et al (San Francisco: Ignatius Press, 1986), II, 514. See R.V. Young, "Chesterton's Paradoxes and Thomist Ontology," *Renascence* 49 (1996): 67-77.

7. Quoted by G. Douglas Atkinson, *Reading Deconstruction: Deconstructive Reading* (Lexington: University Press of Kentucky, 1983), p. 36.

8. *The Order of Things: An Archaeology of the Human Sciences* (New York: Random House, 1970), p. xxiii. See above, Chapter 4, p. 89.

9. Consider not only *Roe v. Wade* (1973) but also *Griswold v. Connecticut* (1965), the contraceptives case in which the Court first conjured the right to privacy out of the magic hat of the fourteenth amendment; or the various rulings mandating "affirma-

tive action" with specific numerical "goals" on the basis of the 1964 Civil Rights Act, which expressly forbids racial quotas in hiring, admissions, and the like.

10. Ronald Dworkin, "Law as Interpretation," *Critical Inquiry* 9 (1982): 179-200; Stanley Fish, "Working on the Chain Gang: Interpretation in the Law and Literary Criticism," ibid., 201-16. Dworkin has reprinted his essay under the title, "How the Law Is Like Literature," in *A Matter of Principle* (Cambridge, MA: Harvard University Press, 1985), pp. 146-66; Fish has repreintd his essay in *Doing What Comes Naturally: Change, Rhetoric, and the Practice of Theory in Literary and Legal Studies* (Durham and London: Duke University Press, 1989), pp. 87-102. I cite the latter versions of each.

11. *Criticism and Social Change* (Chicago: University of Chicago Press, 1984), p. 141.

12. The essay first appeared in the *Sewanee Review* 57 (1949). I quote the version reprinted in W.K. Wimsatt, Jr., *The Verbal Icon: Studies in the Meaning of Poetry* (Lexington: University of Kentucky Press, 1954), p. 21. Along with "The Intentional Fallacy," also written in collaboration with Beardsley and also reprinted in *The Verbal Icon*, the essay comes as close to definitive demonstration as is possible in the humanities.

13. "Literature in the Reader: Affective Stylistics," which first appeared in *New Literary History* (1970), is here quoted from Stanley Fish, *Is There a Text in This Class? The Authority of Interpretive Communities* (Cambridge, MA, and London: Harvard University Press, 1980), p. 23.

14. *Is There a Text in This Class?*, p. 304.

15. *Doing What Comes Naturally*, p. 320.

16. Ibid., p. 326.

17. Ibid., pp. 331-32.

18. Ibid., p. 323.

19. *Is There a Text in This Class?*, p. 319.

20. *Doing What Comes Naturally*, p. 338.

21. *Is There a Text in This Class?*, p. 354.

22. See above Chapter 2, esp. pp. 36-40. Fish's ideas about the relationship between words and their contexts also owes a great deal to the speech-act theories of J.L. Austin and John Searle. See Fish, "How To Do Things with Austin and Searle," *Is There a Text in This Class?*, pp. 197-245.

23. *Is There a Text in This Class?*, p. 305.

24. St. Thomas Aquinas, *The Collected Works of G.K. Chesterton*, II, 515-16. C.S. Lewis makes essentially the same point in *The Abolition of Man* (1947; rpt. New York: Collier Books, 1962), esp. pp. 39-63, about morality: without self-evident moral principles, no moral reasoning is possible.

25. *Is There a Text in This Class?*, p. 368. See above, Chapter 1, pp. 21-22, for the context of this quotation.

26. *Criticism and Social Change*, p. 142.

27. Ibid., p. 359.

28. Ibid., p. 338.

29. Perhaps the best example would be revisionist versions of Shakespeare: feminist productions of *The Taming of the Shrew*, in which Petruccio, rather than Kate, is "tamed," blatantly anti-war productions of *Henry V*, and so on.

30. "Change," in *Doing What Comes Naturally*, p. 141.
31. Ibid., p. 142.
32. Ibid., p. 150.
33. *St. Thomas Aquinas, Collected Works of Chesterton*, II, 530.
34. "Change," *Doing What Comes Naturally*, p. 145.
35. Ibid., p. 146.
36. Ibid., p. 160.
37. "Consequences," *Doing What Comes Naturally*, pp. 323-24.
38. "How Law Is Like Literature," *A Matter of Principle*, p. 146.
39. Ibid., p. 150.
40. Ibid., p. 160.
41. "Working on the Chain Gang," *Doing What Comes Naturally*, p. 88.
42. Dworkin, "How Law Is Like Literature," *A Matter of Principle*, pp. 150-51; Fish, "Working on the Chain Gang," *Doing What Comes Naturally*, pp. 95-97.
43. "On Interpretation and Objectivity," *A Matter of Principle*, p. 174.
44. See F. C. Copleston, *A History of Medieval Philosophy* (New York: Harper & Row, 1972), pp. 206-07; Ralph McInerny, ed. and trans., *Aquinas Against the Averroists: On There Being Only One Intellect* (West Lafayette, IN: Purdue University Press, 1993), pp. 212-13.
45. *De Unitate Intellectus Contra Averroistas*, in *Opuscula Philosophica*, ed. R. Spiazzi (Turin and Rome: Marietti, 1954), #267: "per rationem concludo de necessitate, quod intellectus est unus numero; firmiter tamen teneo oppositum per fidem."
46. "Liberalism," *A Matter of Principle*, p. 191.
47. "Why Liberals Should Care About Equality," ibid., p. 205.
48. Eva R. Rubin, *Abortion, Politics and the Courts*: Roe v. Wade *and Its Aftermath* (Westport, CT: Greenwood Press, 1982), p. 2.
49. See the Symposium, "The End of Democracy? The Judicial Usurpation of Politics," *First Things* #67 (Novermber, 1996): 18-42.
50. Plato, *Republic* 338c.

CHAPTER SIX

1. "To the memory of my beloved, the AUTHOR, MASTER WILLIAM SHAKESPEARE, AND what he hath left us," in William Shakespeare, *The Complete Works*, ed. Stanley Wells and Gary Taylor (Oxford: Clarendon Press, 1988), p. xiv.
2. *Pro Archia Poeta Oratio* I.2, *Selections from Cicero*, ed. Charles E. Bennett (1922; rpt. Boston: Allyn & Bacon, 1968), p. 93: "Etenim omnes artes, quae ad humanitatem pertinent, habent quoddam commune vinculum et quasi cognatione quadam inter se continentur."
3. "Limelight: Reflections on a Public Year," *PMLA* 104 (1989): 286, 287.
4. *Selected Essays* (New York: Harcourt, Brace & World, 1960), p. 5.
5. *Criticism and Social Change* (Chicago: University of Chicago Press, 1984), p. 152. See above, Chapter 1, p. 21.
6. See above, Chapter 4, pp. 92-96.

7. "Last Will and Testament of an Ex-Literary Critic," *Lingua Franca* (September/ October, 1996): 60. For a prominent example of misreading Conrad, see Chinua Achebe, "An Image of Africa: Racism in Conrad's *Heart of Darkness*," in *Heart of Darkness: An Authoritative Text, Backgrounds and Sources, Criticism*, ed. Robert Kimbrough (3rd ed., New York: Norton, 1988), pp. 251-62. Although Kimbrough also publishes partial defenses of Conrad by Wilson Harris (pp. 262-68) and C. P. Sarvan (pp. 280-85, as well as another attack by Frances B. Singh, pp. 268-80), the notable fact is that an editor should feel it necessary to publish Achebe's fatuous and inept misinterpretation in the first place.

8. "West of Everything," *South Atlantic Quarterly* 86 (1987): pp. 375, 376.

9. *Is There a Text in This Class? The Authority of Interpretive Communities* (Cambridge, MA: Harvard University Press, 1980), p. 368. See above, Chapter 1, pp. 21-22.

10. P. 3. "Not a Good Idea" is a six-page, computer-generated document ascribed to Steven Cohan et al, members of the English Department at Syracuse, dated December, 1988. Page numbers of subsequent quotations appear parenthetically in the text.

11. Elizabeth D. Harvey and Katherine Eisaman Maus, ed., *Soliciting Interpretation: Literary Theory and Seventeenth-Century English Poetry* (Chicago: University of Chicago Press, 1990), p. xxi.

12. *There's No Such Thing as Free Speech and It's a Good Thing, Too* (New York and Oxford: Oxford University Press, 1994), p. 41.

13. *Literary Theory: An Introduction* (Minneapolis: University of Minnesota Press, 1983), p. 35.

14. *The Idea of a University*, ed. Martin J. Svaglic (1960; rpt. Notre Dame, IN, and London: University of Notre Dame Press, 1982), p. 91.

15. *The Works of Anne Bradstreet*, ed. Jeannine Hensley (Cambridge, MA and London: Harvard University Press, 1967), p. 224. The baneful effects of ideological obsession are exemplified in this volume by Adrienne Rich's "Foreword" and a "Postscript" subsequently added to later printings. The original "Foreword" provides a brief but respectful account of Bradstreet's grand achievement in producing admirable poetry "while rearing eight children, lying frequently sick, keeping house at the edge of wilderness (p. xx)"; the "Postscript" is largely devoted to Rich herself and what she perceives as the insufficient deference granted her by "white American male writers" (p. xxi). Bradstreet is only important as a putative proto-feminist.

16. Wigglesworth is quoted from *Seventeenth-Century American Poetry*, ed. Harrison T. Meserole (New York: New York University Press, 1968).

17. *The Complete Poems of Emily Dickinson*, ed. Thomas H. Johnson (Boston: Little, Brown & Co., 1957), #712.

18. *Pro Archia Poeta* VI.12: "Qui suppeditat nobis, ubi et animus ex hoc forensi strepitu reficiatur et aures convicio defessae conquiescant."

19. Ibid. VI.14: "Nam, nisi multorum praeceptis multisque litteris mihi ab adulescentia suasissem nihil esse in vita magno opere expetendum nisi laudem atque honestatem, in ea autem persequenda omnes cruciatus corporis, omnia pericula mortis atque exsili parvi esse ducenda, numquam me pro salute vestra in tot ac tantas dimicationes atque in hos profligatorum hominum cottidianos impetus objecissem."

20. Ibid. IX-X passim.

21. Ibid. VII.16: "Nam ceterae neque temporum sunt neque aetatum omnium neque locorum; at haec studia adulescentiam alunt, senectutem oblectant, secundas res ornant, adversis perfugium ac solacium praebent, delectant domi, non impediunt foris, pernoctant nobiscum, peregrinantur, rusticantur."

22. Ibid. VI.14: "Quam multas nobis imagines non solum ad intuendum, verum etiam ad imitandum fortissimorum virorum expressas scriptores et Graeci et Latini reliquerunt!"

23. "The Function of Criticism at the Present Time," *Poetry and Criticism of Matthew Arnold*, ed. A. Dwight Culler (Boston: Houghton Mifflin, 1961), p. 257.

Bibliography

Abrams, M.H. *Natural Supernaturalism: Tradition and Revolution in Romantic Literature*. New York: W.W. Norton & Co., 1971.

Achebe, Chinua. "An Image of Africa: Racism in Conrad's *Heart of Darkness*. In Joseph Conrad. *Heart of Darkness: An Authoritative Text, Backgrounds and Sources, Criticism*. Ed. Robert Kimbrough. 3rd Ed. New York and London: W.W. Norton & Co., 1988, pp. 251-62.

Aers, David and Gunther Kress. "The Language of the Social Order: Individual and Historical Process in *King Lear*." In David Aers, Bob Hodge, and Gunther Kress. *Literature, Language and Society in England, 1580-1680*. Totowa, NJ: Barnes & Noble, 1981.

Aquinas, Saint Thomas. *De Unitate Intellectus Contra Averroistas*. In *Opuscula Philosophica*. Ed. R. Spiazzi. Turin and Rome: Marietti, 1954.

_____. *De Veritate Catholicae Fidei Contra Gentiles*. 2nd Ed. Paris: Bloud et Barral, 1882.

_____. *Quaestiones Disputatae*. 5 vols. in 2. 5th Ed. Turin and Rome: Marietti, 1927.

Arnold, Matthew. *Poetry and Criticism of Matthew Arnold*. Ed. A. Dwight Culler. Boston: Houghton Mifflin, 1961.

Atkinson, G. Douglas. *Reading Deconstruction: Deconstructive Reading.* Lexington: University Press of Kentucky, 1983.

Augustinus, Sanctus Aurelius. *Opera Omnia.* In *Patrologia Latina.* Ed. J. P. Migne. Paris, 1844-55,1862-65, vols. 32-47.

Balthasar, Hans Urs von. *Convergences to the Source of Christian Mystery.* Trans. E.A. Nelson. San Francisco: Ignatius Press, 1983.

Belsey, Catherine. *Critical Practice.* London and New York: Methuen, 1980.

Berger, Raoul. "Justice Brennan Is Wrong." *Human Life Review* 12 (1986), No. 1:106-08.

Bloom, Allan. *The Closing of the American Mind.* New York: Simon & Schuster, 1987.

Bloom, Harold. *Agon: Towards a Theory of Literary Revisionism.* New York and Oxford: Oxford University Press, 1982.

_____. "The Breaking of Form." In *Deconstruction and Criticism.* New York: Seabury Press, 1979, pp. 1-37.

_____. *The Breaking of the Vessels.* Chicago and London: University of Chicago Press, 1982.

_____. *Wallace Stevens: The Poems of Our Climate.* Ithaca, NY, and London: Cornell University Press, 1977.

Bradstreet, Anne. *The Works of Anne Bradstreet.* Ed. Jeannine Hensley. Foreword Adrienne Rich. Cambridge, MA, and London: Harvard University Press, 1967.

Brazeau, Peter. *Parts of a World: Wallace Stevens Remembered: An Oral Biography.* New York: Random House, 1983.

Brooks, Cleanth. *Historical Evidence and the Reading of Seventeenth-Century Poetry.* Columbia and London: University of Missouri Press, 1991.

_____. "Irony as a Principle of Structure." In *Literary Opinion in America.* Ed. Morton Dauwen Zabel. 3rd Ed. New York: Harper & Row, 1962, II, 729-41.

_____. *The Well Wrought Urn: Studies in the Structure of Poetry.* New York: Harcourt, Brace & World, 1947.

_____ and Robert Penn Warren. *Understanding Poetry.* New York: Holt, Rinehart & Winston, 1938.

Burgum, Edwin Berry, Ed. *The New Criticism: An Anthology of Modern Aesthetics and Literary Criticism.* New York: Prentice-Hall, 1930.

Cain, William. *The Crisis in Criticism: Theory, Literature, and Reform in English Studies.* Baltimore and London: Johns Hopkins University Press, 1984.

Cartelli, Thomas. "Prospero in Africa: *The Tempest* as Colonialist Text and Pretext." In *Shakespeare Reproduced: The Text in History and Ideology.* Ed. Jean E. Howard and Marion F. O'Connor. New York and London: Methuen, 1987, pp. 99-115.

Chesterton, G.K. *Saint Thomas Aquinas.* 1933. Rpt. *The Collected Works of G.K. Chesterton.* Vol. II. Ed. George J. Marlin et al. San Francisco: Ignatius Press, 1986.

Cicero, Marcus Tullius. *Selections from Cicero.* Ed. Charles E. Bennett. 1922. Rpt. Boston: Allyn & Bacon, 1968.

Cohan, Steve et al. *Not a Good Idea: A New Curriculum at Syracuse.* Unpublished document attributed to members of the English Department of Syracuse University, December, 1988.

Copleston, F.C. *A History of Medieval Philosophy.* New York: Harper & Row, 1972.

Culler, Jonathan. *On Deconstruction: Theory and Criticism After Structuralism.* Ithaca, NY: Cornell University Press, 1982.

_____. *The Pursuit of Signs: Semiotics, Literature, Deconstruction.* Ithaca, NY: Cornell University Press, 1981.

Danby, John F. *Shakespeare's Doctrine of Nature: A Study of* King Lear. London: Faber & Faber, 1948.

de Man, Paul. *Blindness and Insight: Essays in Contemporary Rhetoric.* Intro. Wlad Godzich. 2nd Rev. Ed. Minneapolis: University of

Minnesota Press, 1983.

_____."Shelley Disfigured." In *Deconstruction and Criticism*. New York: Seabury Press, 1979, pp. 39–73.

Denzinger, Henr. and Clem. Bannwort, S.J. *Enchiridion Symbolorum, Definitionum et Declarationum*. 17th Ed. Friburgi Brigoviae: Herder & Co., 1928.

Derrida, Jacques. *Dissemination*. Trans. Barbara Johnson. Chicago: University of Chicago Press, 1981.

_____. "Like the Sound of the Sea Deep within a Shell." *Critical Inquiry* 14 (1988): 591–652.

_____. *Margins of Philosophy*. Trans. Alan Bass. Chicago: University of Chicago Press, 1982.

_____. *Of Grammatology*. Trans. Gayatri Chakravorty Spivak. Baltimore and London: Johns Hopkins University Press, 1976.

_____. *Positions*. Trans. Alan Bass. Chicago: University of Chicago Press, 1981.

_____. *Speech and Phenomena and Other Essays on Husserl's Theory of Signs*. Trans. David B. Allison. Evanston, IL: Northwestern University Press, 1973.

_____. "Structure, Sign, and Play in the Discourse of the Human Sciences." In *The Structuralist Controversy: The Language of Criticism and the Sciences of Man*. Ed. Richard Macksey and Eugenio Donato. Baltimore and London: Johns Hopkins University Press, 1970, pp. 247–72.

_____. *Writing and Difference*. Trans. Alan Bass. Chicago: University of Chicago Press, 1978.

Dickinson, Emily. *The Complete Poems of Emily Dickinson*. Ed. Thomas H. Johnson. Boston and Toronto: Little, Brown & Co., 1957.

The Dissolution of General Education, 1914-1993. Princeton, NJ: National Association of Scholars, 1996.

Donne, John. *The Complete Poetry of John Donne*. Ed. John T. Shawcross.

Garden City, NY: Doubleday & Co., 1967.

Dowden, Edward. "Introduction." In *The Poetical Works of Shelley*. New York: Thomas Crowell, n.d.

Dubrow, Heather. *Echoes of Desire: English Petrarchism and Its Counterdiscourses*. Ithaca and London: Cornell University Press, 1995.

_____ and Richard Strier, Eds. "Introduction: The Historical Renaissance." In *The Historical Renaissance: New Essays on Tudor and Stuart Culture*. Chicago and London: University of Chicago Press, 1988, pp. 1-12.

Dworkin, Ronald. *A Matter of Principle*. Cambridge, MA, and London: Harvard University Press, 1985.

Eagleton, Terry. *Literary Theory: An Introduction*. Minneapolis: University of Minnesota Press, 1983.

_____. *Marxism and Literary Criticism*. Berkeley and Los Angeles: University of California Press, 1976.

Eliot, T.S. *Selected Essays*. New York: Harcourt, Brace & World, 1960.

Ellis, John M. *Against Deconstruction*. Princeton, NJ: Princeton University Press, 1989.

_____. *Literature Lost: Social Agendas and the Corruption of the Humanities*. New Haven and London: Yale University Press, 1997.

"The End of Democracy? The Judicial Usurpation of Politics." *First Things* #67 (November, 1996): 18-42.

Fish, Stanley. *Doing What Comes Naturally: Change, Rhetoric, and the Practice of Theory in Literary and Legal Studies*. Durham, NC, and London: Duke University Press, 1989.

_____. *Is There a Text in This Class? The Authority of Interpretive Communities*. Cambridge, MA, and London: Harvard University Press, 1980.

_____. *There's No Such Thing as Free Speech and It's a Good Thing, Too*. New York and Oxford: Oxford University Press, 1994.

Foucault, Michel. *The Foucault Reader*. Ed. Paul Rabinow. New York: PantheonBooks, 1984.

_____. *The Order of Things: An Archaeology of the Human Sciences*. 1970. Rpt. New York: Vintage Books, 1973.

Fox-Genovese, Elizabeth. *Feminism Is Not the Story of My Life: How Today's Feminist Elite Has Lost Touch with the Real Concerns of Women*. New York: Nan A. Talese, 1996.

Frye, Northrop. *Anatomy of Criticism: Four Essays*. Princeton, NJ: Princeton University Press, 1957.

Gallop, Jane. *Reading Lacan*. Ithaca, NY, and London: Cornell University Press, 1985.

Gates, Henry Louis, Jr. *Loose Canons: Notes on the Culture Wars*. New York and Oxford: Oxford University Press, 1992.

Graff, Gerald. *Literature Against Itself: Literary Ideas in Modern Society*. Chicago and London: University of Chicago Press, 1979.

Greenblatt, Stephen. *Renaissance Self-Fashioning from More to Shakespeare*. Chicago and London: University of Chicago Press, 1980.

_____. *Shakespearean Negotiations: The Circulation of Social Energy in Renaissance England*. Berkeley and Los Angeles: University of California Press, 1988.

Hall, Kim. *Things of Darkness: Economies of Race and Gender in Early Modern England*. Ithaca, NY, and London: Cornell University Press, 1995.

Harris, Wilson. "The Frontier on Which the *Heart of Darkness* Stands." In Joseph Conrad. *Heart of Darkness: An Authoritative Text, Backgrounds and Sources, Criticism*. Ed. Robert Kimbrough. 3rd Ed. New York and London: W. W. Norton & Co., 1988, pp. 262-68.

Hartman, Geoffrey H., Ed. "Preface." In *Psychoanalysis and the Question of the Text*. Baltimore and London: Johns Hopkins University Press, 1978, pp. vii-xix.

Harvey, Elizabeth D. and Katherine Eisaman Maus, Eds. "Introduction." In *Soliciting Interpretation: Literary Theory and Seventeenth-Century English Poetry*. Chicago and London: University of Chicago Press, 1988, pp. ix-xxiii.

Hassan, Ihab. *Paracriticisms: Seven Speculations of the Times*. Urbana, Chicago, London: University of Illinois Press, 1975.

Hirsch, David. *The Deconstruction of Literature: Criticism After Auschwitz*. Hanover, NH, and London: University Press of New England, 1991.

Hirsch, E. D. *Cultural Literacy: What Every American Needs to Know*. Boston: Houghton Mifflin, 1987.

Hobbes, Thomas. *Leviathan*. Ed. C.B. Macpherson. Harmondsworth: Penguin Books, 1968.

Howard, Jean E. and Marion F. O'Connor, Eds. "Introduction." In *Shakespeare Reproduced: The Text in History and Ideology*. New York and London: Methuen, 1987, pp. 1-17.

Hutcheon, Linda. *Irony's Edge: The Theory and Politics of Irony*. London and New York: Routledge, 1994.

Ingarden, Roman. *The Literary Work of Art: An Investigation on the Borderlines of Ontology, Logic, and Theory of Literature*. Trans. George G. Grabowicz. Evanston, IL: Northwestern University Press, 1973.

Jaki, Stanley L. *The Road of Science and the Ways to God*. Chicago: University of Chicago Press, 1978.

Jameson, Fredric. *The Prison-House of Language: A Critical Account of Structuralism and Russian Formalism*. Princeton, NJ: Princeton University Press, 1972.

Jed, Stephanie H. *Chaste Thinking: The Rape of Lucretia and the Birth of Humanism*. Bloomington and Indianapolis: Indiana University Press, 1989.

Johnson, Barbara. "The Frame of Reference: Poe, Lacan, and Derrida." In *Psychoanalysis and the Question of the Text*. Ed. Geoffrey

H. Hartman. Baltimore and London: Johns Hopkins University Press, 1978, pp. 149-71.

_____. *A World of Difference*. Baltimore and London: Johns Hopkins University Press, 1989.

Kant, Immanuel. *Prolegomena to Any Future Metaphysics*. Trans. Paul Carus. 1902 Rpt. LaSalle, IL: Opencourt, 1967.

Jones, E. Michael. "Metaphysics as Tarbaby: Intention, Deconstruction, and Absolutes." *Center Journal* 1 (1982), No. 2: 9-37.

Lacan, Jacques. *Feminine Sexuality: Jacques Lacan and the école freudienne*. Ed. Juliet Mitchell and Jacqueline Rose. Trans. Jacqueline Rose. New York and London: W.W. Norton & Co., 1985.

_____. "Of Structure as an Inmixing of an Otherness Prerequisite to Any Subject Whatsoever." In *The Structuralist Controversy: The Languages of Criticism and the Sciences of Man*. Ed. Richard Macksey and Eugenio Donato. Baltimore and London: Johns Hopkins University Press, 1972, pp. 186-200.

Lehman, David. *Signs of the Times: Deconstruction and the Fall of Paul de Man*. New York: Poseidon Press, 1991.

Lentricchia, Frank. *After the New Criticism*. Chicago: University of Chicago Press, 1980.

_____. *Ariel and the Police: Michel Foucault, William James, Wallace Stevens*. Madison: University of Wisconsin Press, 1988.

_____. *Criticism and Social Change*. Chicago: University of Chicago Press, 1984.

_____. "Last Will and Testament of an Ex-Literary Critic." *Lingua Franca*. (September/October, 1996): 59-67.

Levin, Samuel. *Metaphoric Worlds: Conceptions of a Romantic Nature*. New Haven and London: Yale University Press, 1988.

Lewis, C.S. *The Abolition of Man*. 1947. Rpt. New York: Collier Books, 1962.

_____ and E. M. W. Tillyard. *The Personal Heresy*. London: Oxford

University Press, 1939.

Magliola, Robert. *Derrida on the Mend.* West Lafayette, IN: Purdue University Press, 1984.

McFadden, J.P. "Introduction." *Human Life Review* 12 (1986), No. 1: 2-6.

McInerny, Ralph, Ed. and Trans. *Aquinas Against the Averroists: On There Being Only One Intellect.* West Lafayette, IN: Purdue University Press, 1993.

Melville, Stephen. *Philosophy Beside Itself: On Deconstruction and Modernism.* Minneapolis: University of Minnesota Press, 1986.

Miel, Jan. "Jacques Lacan and the Structure of the Unconscious." In *Structuralism.* Ed. Jacques Ehrmann. Garden City, NY: Doubleday Anchor, 1970, pp. 94-101.

Miller, J. Hillis. "The Critic as Host." In *Deconstruction and Criticism.* New York: Seabury Press, 1979, pp. 217-53.

Mitchell, Juliet. "Introduction—I." In *Feminine Sexuality: Jacques Lacan and the école Freudienne.* New York and London: W.W. Norton & Co., 1985, pp. 1-26.

Newman, John Henry. *The Idea of a University.* Ed. Martin J. Svaglic. 1960. Rpt. Notre Dame, IN, and London: University of Notre Dame Press, 1982.

Nietzsche, Friedrich. *The Birth of Tragedy and the Genealogy of Morals.* Trans. Francis Golffing. Garden City, NY: Doubleday & Co., 1966.

O'Connor, Flannery. *Collected Works.* Ed. Sally Fitzgerald. New York: Library of America, 1988.

_____. *Mystery and Manners.* Ed. Sally and Robert Fitzgerald. New York: Farrar, Strauss & Giroux, 1966.

Pagels, Elaine. *The Gnostic Gospels.* 1979. Rpt. New York: Vintage Books, 1981.

Pelikan, Jaroslav. *The Christian Tradition: A History of the Development of Doctrine.* Vol. I: *The Emergence of the Catholic Tradition (100-600).*

Chicago: University of Chicago Press, 1971.

Perrine, Laurence J. *Sound and Sense.* New York: Harcourt, Brace & World, 1956.

Plato. *Republic.* Ed. and Trans. Paul Shorey. 2 Vols. Cambridge, MA: Harvard University Press, 1930, 1935.

Ransom, John Crowe. *The New Criticism.* New York: New Directions, 1941.

_____. *The World's Body.* 1938. Rpt. Baton Rouge: Louisiana State University Press, 1968.

Ray, William. *Literary Meaning: From Phenomenology to Deconstruction.* Oxford: Basil Blackwell, 1984.

Richards, I.A. *Principles of Literary Criticism.* 3rd Ed. New York: Harcourt, Brace & World, 1956.

Richardson, Joan. *Wallace Stevens: The Later Years, 1923-1955.* New York: William Morrow, 1988.

Rose, Jacqueline. "Introduction—II." In *Feminine Sexuality: Jacques Lacan and the école Freudienne.* New York and London: W.W. Norton & Co., 1985, pp. 27-57.

Rubin, Eva R. *Abortion, Politics and the Courts: Roe v. Wade and Its Aftermath.* Westport, CT: Greenwood Press, 1982.

Said, Edward W. *The World, the Text, and the Critic.* Cambridge, MA: Harvard University Press, 1983.

Sarvan, C.P. "Racism and the *Heart of Darkness.*" In Joseph Conrad. *Heart of Darkness: An Authoritative Text, Backgrounds and Sources, Criticism.* Ed. Robert Kimbrough. 3rd Ed. New York and London: W.W. Norton & Co., 1988, pp. 280-85.

Saussure, Ferdinand de. *Course in General Linguistics.* Trans. Wade Baskin. 1959. Rpt. New York: McGraw Hill, 1966.

Selden, Raman. *A Reader's Guide to Contemporary Literary Theory.* Lexington: University Press of Kentucky, 1985.

Shakespeare, William. *The Complete Works: Compact Edition.* Ed. Stanley

Wells and Gary Taylor. Oxford: Clarendon Press, 1988.

Shuger, Debora. "Castigating Livy: The Rape of Lucretia and *The Old Arcadia.*" *Renaissance Quarterly* 51 (1998): 526-48.

Sidney, Sir Philip. *An Apology for Poetry.* In *Elizabethan Critical Essays.* Ed. G. Gregory Smith. 2 Vols. London: Oxford University Press, 1904, I, 150-207.

Singh, Frances B. "The Colonialist Bias of *Heart of Darkness.*" In Joseph Conrad. *Heart of Darkness: An Authoritative Text, Backgrounds and Sources, Criticism.* Ed. Robert Kimbrough. 3rd Ed. New York and London: W.W. Norton & Co., 1988, pp. 268-80.

Smith, Barbara Herrnstein. "Limelight: Reflections on a Public Year." *PMLA* 104 (1989): 285-93.

Smith, Johanna. "'Too Beautiful Altogether': Patriarchal Ideology in *Heart of Darkness.*" In Joseph Conrad. *Heart of Darkness: A Case Study in Contemporary Criticism.* Ed. Ross C. Murfin. New York: St. Martin's Press, 1989, pp. 179-95.

Sobran, Joseph. "Forgotten Checks and Balances." *Human Life Review* 12 (1986), No. 1: 104-05.

_____. "Principle and Power: Abortion, the Court, and Federalism." *Human Life Review* 12 (1986), No. 1: 17-29.

Sommers, Christina Hoff. *Who Stole Feminism? How Women Have Betrayed Women.* New York: Simon & Schuster, 1994.

Stevens, Wallace. *The Collected Poems of Wallace Stevens.* New York: Alfred Knopf, 1954.

_____. *The Palm at the End of the Mind: Selected Poems and a Play.* Ed. Holly Stevens. New York: Random House, 1972.

Tallis, Raymond. *Not Saussure: A Critique of Post-Saussurian Literary Theory.* 2nd Ed. New York: St. Martin's Press, 1995.

Taylor, Mark C. *Erring: A Postmodern A/Theology.* Chicago and London: University of Chicago Press, 1984.

Thompson, Ewa. "Dialectical Methodologies in the American Academy." *Modern Age* 28 (1984), No. 1: 9–22.

Tompkins, Jane. "West of Everything." *South Atlantic Quarterly* 86 (1987): 357–77.

Virgil. *Eclogues*. Ed. and Trans. Guy Lee. Rev. Ed. Harmondsworth: Penguin Books, 1984.

Voegelin, Eric. *The New Science of Politics: An Introduction*. 1952. Rpt. Chicago and London: University of Chicago Press, 1987.

Wellek, René. *The Attack on Literature and Other Essays*. Chapel Hill: University of North Carolina Press, 1982.

_____ and Austin Warren. *Theory of Literature*. 3rd Ed. New York: Harcourt, Brace & World, 1956.

Wigglesworth, Michael. *The Day of Doom*. In *Seventeenth-Century American Poetry*. Ed. Harrison T. Meserole. New York: New York University Press, 1968.

Wimsatt, William K., Jr. *The Day of the Leopards: Essays in Defense of Poems*. New Haven and London: Yale University Press, 1976.

_____. *The Verbal Icon: Studies in the Meaning of Poetry*. Lexington: University of Kentucky Press, 1954.

Wordsworth, William. *The Prose Works of William Wordsworth*. Ed. A.B. Grosart. 3 Vols. London, 1876.

Young, R.V. "Chesterton's Paradoxes and Thomist Ontology." *Renascence* 49 (1996): 67–77.

Index